The Year of the Poet XI

October 2024

The Poetry Posse

inner child press, ltd.
'building bridges of cultural understanding'

The Poetry Posse 2024

Gail Weston Shazor
Shareef Abdur Rasheed
Teresa E. Gallion
hülya n. yılmaz
Noreen Snyder
Tzemin Ition Tsai
Elizabeth Esguerra Castillo
Jackie Davis Allen
Mutawaf Shaheed
Caroline 'Ceri' Nazareno
Ashok K. Bhargava
Alicja Maria Kuberska
Swapna Behera
Albert 'Infinite' Carrasco
Michelle Joan Barulich
Eliza Segiet
William S. Peters, Sr.

~ * ~

In order to maintain each poet's authentic voice, this volume has not undergone the scrutiny of editing. Please take time to indulge each contributor for their own creativity and aspirations to convey their uniqueness.

hülya n. yılmaz, Ph.D.
Director of Editing ~
Inner Child Press International

General Information

The Year of the Poet XI

October 2024 Edition

The Poetry Posse

1st Edition : 2024

Publisher Information

1st Edition : Inner Child Press
intouch@innerchildpress.com
www.innerchildpress.com

ISBN-13 : 978-1-961498-43-3 (inner child press, ltd.)

$ 12.99

WHAT WOULD

LIFE

BE WITHOUT

A LITTLE

POETRY?

Dedication

This Book is dedicated to

Humanity, Peace & Poetry

the Power of the Pen

can effectuate change!

&

The Poetry Posse

past, present & future,

our Patrons and Readers &

the Spirit of our Everlasting Muse

In the darkness of my life
I heard the music
I danced . . .
and the Light appeared
and I dance

Janet P. Caldwell

Table of Contents

The Poetry Posse

Table of Contents . . . *continued*

Foreword

Renowned Poets

Adam Bernard Mickiewicz

Adam Mickiewicz is one of the foremost poets of Polish Romanticism and a pivotal figure in Poland's literary and political history. Born in 1798 in Nowogródek, then part of the Polish-Lithuanian Commonwealth (now in Belarus), Mickiewicz lived during the turbulent period of Poland's partition and loss of sovereignty. This historical backdrop profoundly influenced his thoughts and infused his literary works, making him a symbol of the Polish national spirit.

Mickiewicz's works are imbued with patriotism, romanticism, and religious fervor—elements that define his poetry and plays. As a pioneer of Polish Romanticism, his literary creations focus on freedom, personal heroism, and Poland's yearning for independence. His poetry often weaves together vivid depictions of nature, mysticism, and folklore, demonstrating a deep emotional intensity and philosophical reflection.

One of his most celebrated works is the epic poem Pan Tadeusz, regarded as one of the most significant literary achievements in Polish literature. Set against the backdrop of Polish nobility, the poem vividly portrays the people's nostalgia and love for their lost homeland in the early 19th century, while also expressing their desire for Poland's revival. Praised as a masterpiece of Polish literature, Pan Tadeusz carries not only historical value but also Mickiewicz's profound attachment to his homeland and the Polish national spirit.

In addition to Pan Tadeusz, another of Mickiewicz's key works is Dziady (often translated as Forefathers' Eve). This dramatic piece blends Polish folklore with Christian beliefs, delving into themes of life, death, and the salvation of souls. The play serves as an allegory for Poland's suffering and emphasizes spiritual and national liberation, further solidifying Mickiewicz's status as a revered poet and national icon.

Mickiewicz was not only a poet but also an active political figure. He supported Poland's national liberation movements and, during his exile in France, Italy, and Turkey, continuously worked toward the cause of Polish freedom. Like many Polish patriots of the 19th century, Mickiewicz intertwined his creative work with his political ideals, becoming a symbol of the Polish independence movement.

Though Mickiewicz passed away in 1855, his literary legacy continues to influence Polish culture and literature lovers worldwide. His works not only express profound personal emotions but also reflect the history and spiritual aspirations of the entire Polish nation. To this day, his poetry stands as a testament to the unwavering Polish desire for freedom and independence, and it remains a cornerstone of Poland's national identity.

Prof. Tzemin Ition Tsai
(蔡澤民),Dr.,
Taiwan(China).

Now Available

www.innerchildpress.com/world-healing-world-peace-poetry

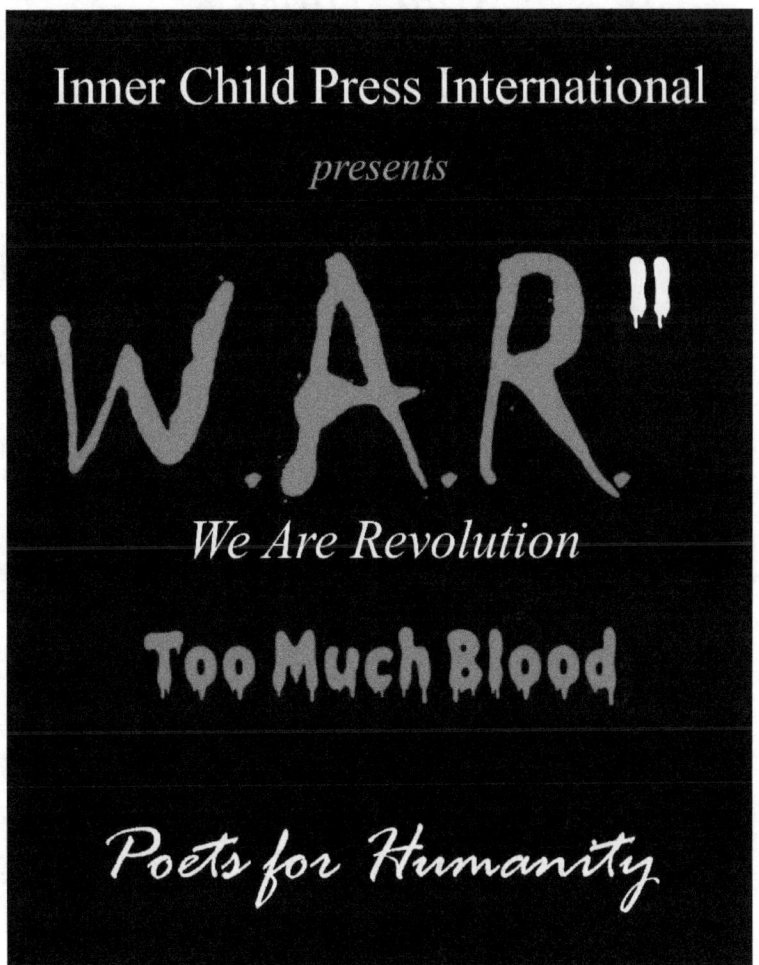

Opening Soon for Submissions
Stay Tuned

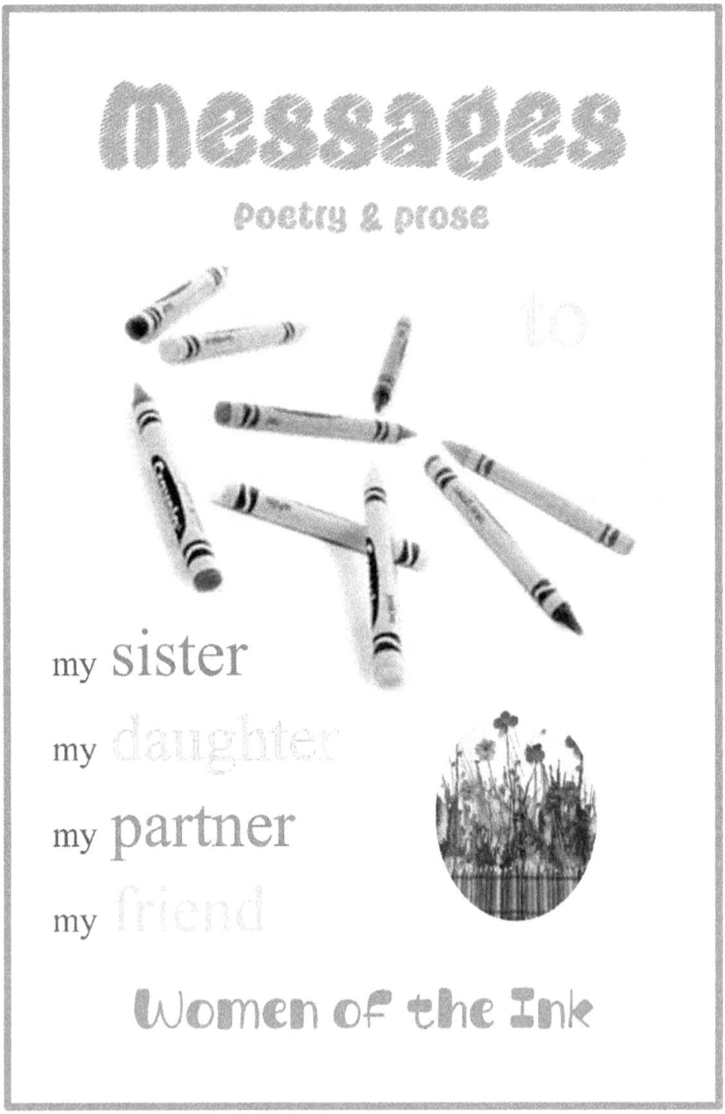

Preface

We, **Inner Child Press International, The Year of the Poet** and **The Poetry Posse** welcome you.

WOW . . . a decade +. We continue to be excited as we are now coming close to finishing our 11th year of Production for **The Year of the Poet**. It just keeps getting better!

This particular year we have chosen to feature renowned poets of history. We do hope you enjoy. Read ~ Learn.

For those of you who are not familiar with our story, back in 2013, a few of us poets got together with the simple intention of producing a book a month. That was our challenge. Since that time the enterprise has blossomed and brought forth a fruit that seems to keep on growing as evidenced as we enter 2023.

Our purpose is simple. Through our lyrical words and verse, we not only wish to share our poetic works, but we also have the poetic naiveté to believe that we can assist in the growth of consciousness of the things that have an effect our collective humanity. Therefore, we welcome your readership. For more about what we are attempting to accomplish, have a look at our Publishing Web Site . . . www.innerchildpress.com. If you would like to

know a bit more about this particular endeavor please stop by for a visit at :
www.innerchildpress.com/the-year-of-the-poet

Over the years, Inner Child Press has been socially active to bring awareness and catalog through literature the things that have an impact upon our world and its inhabitants. We have solicited, produced, underwritten and published quite a few volumes to that end. For more insight you may wish to visit : www.innerchildpress.com/the-anthology-market. If you are a writer, poet, or activist, you would be advised to keep a eye out for upcoming volumes should you desire to participate. All readers are welcomed as well. Note, that there is a myriad of published volumes that are available as a FREE PDF download as well as available for purchase at affordable prices.

We at this time extend to you our well wishes for your own personal journey and hope that you consider including us as a travel companion.

Bless Up

Bill

William S. Peters, Sr.

Publisher
Inner Child Press International
www.innerchildpress.com

Renowned Poets
Adam Bernard Mickiewicz

1798 ~ 1855

October 2024

by hülya n. yılmaz, Ph.D.

A lifelong advocate of Polish national freedom, the romantic, poet, translator, and journalist from Poland spent most of his life as a migrant. As a widely traveled individual, the life story of Mickiewicz is, in actuality, one of a transnational nature. He was exiled to Russia in 1824 due to his activities within the Philomath* Society. In Russia, he enjoyed friendly relations with Aleksandr Pushkin and other intellectuals, including Taras Shevchenko. After escaping exile, Mickiewicz embarked on his travels to Germany, Hungary, Switzerland, Italy, and finally, to Konstantinople (today's Istanbul in the Republic of Turkey). The last leg of his journey is claimed to have materialized at the request of Prince Adam Jerzy Czartoryski. Some historical records indicate that he was to establish political connections in Turkey for the prince; yet, only a brief time after his arrival in Constantinople, he died.

At this point, a look at one of the most famed Mickiewicz poems seems to be in order; for, he has been called a 'self-appointed pilgrim, as "The Ackerman Steppe" articulates---"measureless," the poet goes.

The Ackerman Steppe

Across sea-meadows measureless I go,

        My wagon sinking under grass so tall

The flowery petals in foam on me fall,

And blossom-isles float by I do not know.
No pathway can the deepening twilight show;
I seek the beckoning stars which sailors call,
And watch the clouds. What lies there brightening all?
The Dneister's, the steppe-ocean's evening glow!

The silence! I can hear far flight of cranes—
So far, the eyes of an eagle could not reach—
And bees and blossoms speaking each to each;
The serpent slipping adown grassy lanes;
From my far home if word could come to me!—
Yet none will come. On, o'er the meadow-sea!

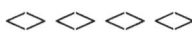

<> <> <> <>

* The Philomaths, “lovers of knowledge,” had formed a secret student association and were active in the capital of Lithuania between 1817 and 1823. They initially constituted a discussion group with a focus on their own work. At the outset of 1819, the group also promoted the idea of Polish independence. The influence of these “lovers of knowledge” on the student scene was significant. Hence, the birth of their offshoots, such as the Philarets or Philadelphists. When their activities became known to the Russian authorities in 1823,

20 Philomats and Philarets were sentenced to death. (From: *Copernico*)

<> <> <> <>

Selected Sources:

Encyclopedia Britannica

Copernico. History and Cultural Heritage in Eastern Europe

CULTURE.PL #language & literature

allpoetry.com

Wikipedia

<> <> <> <>

hülya n. yılmaz, Ph.D.

Professor Emerita, Liberal Arts

(Penn State, U.S.A.)

Director of Editing Services,

Inner Child Press International (U.S.A.)

Poets . . .
sowing seeds in the
Conscious Garden of Life,
that those who have yet to come
may enjoy the Flowers.

Poets, Writers . . . know that we are the enchanting magicians that nourishes the seeds of dreams and thoughts . . . it is our words that entice the hearts and minds of others to believe there is something grand about the possibilities that life has to offer and our words tease it forth into action . . . for you are the Poet, the Writer to whom the Gift of Words has been entrusted . . .

~ wsp

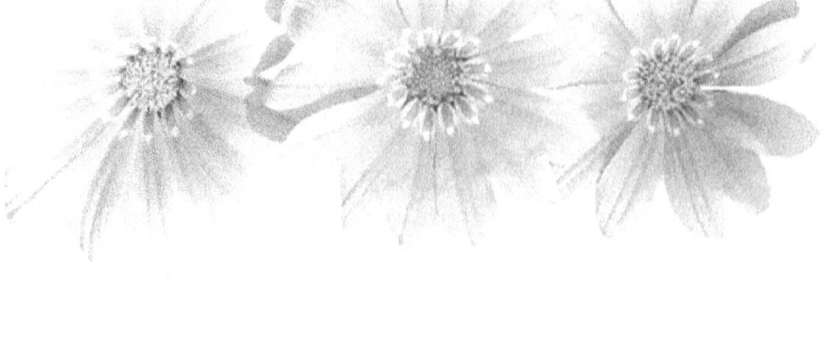

Poetry succeeds where instruction fails.

~ wsp

Now Available

www.innerchildpress.com/the-anthology-market.com

Gail
Weston
Shazor

Gail Weston Shazor is a lover of words. She is fond of the arcane, unusual and the not yet words.

Coining words at an early age, there was often a bit of trouble with teachers, but she always had her mother and aunt to back up her choices in expression. Born in Mississippi, she spent her early years with her grandparents. Each of the four left very careful influences on her pre-schooling. She learned in turn how women worked in and out of the home and how men worked in and out of the home to support the family. She learned that a lack of proper schooling was not the only way to learn and understanding life was a great teacher. As in most rural families of color, women had a greater chance of formal learning. Both of Gail's grandmothers read out loud to the family whether it was the bible or the newspapers and important documents to their spouses.

Gail Weston Shazor has authored (so far) Notes from the Blue Roof, A Overstanding of an Imperfect Love, HeartSongs and Lies My Grandfather's Told Me. The number of anthologies is too many to list with the premier accomplishment of one of the contributors to The Year of The Poet. Gail will always lend her ink to community projects and will purchase the books of fellow poets in the Inner Child Press family.

Sleeping Siren

Genus Capreaetion Sirenum
To add humanness to the mix
Would personify a consciousness
That is fabled has been lost
Over cliff and rocks
And for many moons
You have been quietly watching the sea
Attached to the island of your birth
Or even of your exiled passions

It has been said your longing is palatable
In the crashing waves of oceans
Your song irresistible to those
On whom your eye falls across the tide
He awoke you from the reverie
Of the solitude you share with yourselves
And the words are not enough
So you result to a rhythm of drums
Mimicking the purity of the heart

While your father may be of the sea
Your husband is one of iron
And of them both you seek escape
In a temporal consolation of kisses
To know you are out there waiting
Makes my soul tired of anticipation
Of the next and the next times

Unrivaled of your physical beauty
The rest of us are left to primp
Our characters and integrities

In an effort to be seen in the cleft
Of hidden caves left open to view
Love is never sufficient for mortals
And so we lose the ones we love
To lust such as you embody

Yet, I would not sacrifice who I am
To be one just like you
For you will never leave your
Shackled iron bound ring
For the love of one who you captured
I would only have you stop your song
Long enough to free a heart
For the mere rest of us

hanging up

The blood rushes to my head
And I find it hard to breathe
The aching and pain of a skull
Filled to bursting
With the blood of life
With the
Blood
Of
Death
And the smell
Of pretensions
Wafting through my ears
My ankles ache
From the chaffing of the bindings
Findings
Wanting
Needing
The lessening
From the chains pulling across bones
Stretched to many limits of flesh
If I could just
Touch the ground with my fingertips
I might find a temporary relief
Outside my spirit woman
A tantalizing
And unfulfilling satiation
Much like a laden table with no salt
Tasteless
So I hang
And not as he hung
In perfection
But away from heaven

Unworthy to bear the fruit of a race
Cast into the branches
In places far from
Golgotha
For much the same earthbound reason
Fear
Reflecton
Hate
Each hair shirt heavier than the next
Worn uneasily
In desert heat and verdant forests
In cotton fields and steel mills
Even upside
Down
Here I hang
And my vision is finally clear

VIP

You call to me in peace
And that is what I answer
For you recognize the need
That I currently have
I turn to your healing powers
Of cool, liquid raw greenness
You knew I needed this
From the touch of my hand
And the look in my eyes
I sip the newness across my tongue
Not wanting to gulp the healing
Into my body, my belly, my words
The sweat poured from my nappy hair
Cleaning me, washing my pain
Until water poured from my eyes
Rooted to the floor
Unable to move until I felt
The touch of your arms around me
The quieting shhhs flowing over my skin
And we stood there
The needing and the necessary of life
A possessor of knowledge of ages past
“what else can I do?” you asked me
But my pain was too great to answer
I just didn’t want you
To let me go in that moment
So I placed my hands in yours
Following your calm
You said to me “today this room means
Vessel In Pain” pointing to the VIP sign
And you left me there
In that quiet space
To find my healing

Alicja Maria Kuberska

Alicja Maria Kuberska – awarded Polish poetess, novelist, journalist, editor.

She is a member of the Polish Writers Associations in Warsaw, Poland and IWA Bogdani, Albania. She is also a member of directors' board of Soflay Literature Foundation, Our Poetry Archive (India) and Cultural Ambassador for Poland (Inner Child Press, USA)

Her poems have been published in numerous anthologies and magazines in : Poland, Czech Republic, Slovakia, Hungary,Ukraina, Belgium, Bulgaria, Albania, Spain, the UK, Italy, the USA, Canada, the UK, Argentina, Chile, Peru, Israel, Turkey, India, Uzbekistan, South Korea, Taiwan, China, Australia, South Africa, Zambia, Nigeria

She received two medals - the Nosside UNESCO Competition in Italy (2015) and European Academy of Science Arts and Letters in France (2017). Ahe also received a reward of international literary competition in Italy „ Tra le parole e 'elfinito" (2018). She was announced a poet of the 2017 year by Soflay Literature Foundation (2018).She also received : Bolesław Prus Prize Poland (2019), Culture Animator Poland (2019) and first prize Premio Internazionale di Poesia Poseidonia- Paestrum Italy (2019).

Mr. Thaddeus

For Adam Mickiewicz

From Zaosie to Constantinople, the road is long
full of life's twists and turns,
unfulfilled dreams of the homeland's freedom.
Fickle fate condemned him to wander across Europe and Asia.
It never allowed him to return to his native land,
and inscribed poverty and longing into his life story.
It is this longing that drives his thoughts to wander again
through vast fields covered in white buckwheat,
leading along narrow paths in the ancient forest.
Like an echo, love sighs return,
lingering glances and romantic songs,
memories of happy days in the nobleman's manor.
The lost land of childhood came alive in verse.
The epic poem closed the abyss of quarrels and accusations,
and the heart of the nation beat loudly, strengthened.

The Table

Square, solid
Made by a village carpenter.
On its worn-out surface,
an iron with a slug burnt a heart.
It survived the war's turmoil
and the post-war years of darkness.
It heard conspiratorial whispers,
loud laughter, quiet sorrows.
When needed, it became an ark,
taking on board drowning people.
The table with the heart is gone.
It didn't fit the elegant interior.
It vanished with the smoke straight to the sky,
warming the household with its last breath.

The Chandelier

It bent its seven arms like swan necks
And majestically floated to the white ceiling,
Lighting the darkness with a warm glow.
Transparent water lilies bloomed,
And a rainbow sparkled in the glass crystals.
The Murano masters' work is admired for centuries.
The fragile masterpiece never leaves the ballroom,
It gently trembles, dancing in the wind's embrace.
And when needed, it replaces the sunlight.
Aesthetic like a prima ballerina does pirouettes
From simple forms to intricate shapes.
Beauty is eternal and doesn't fade with fashion
The chandelier knows that time hasn't stolen its charm.

Jackie Davis Allen

Jackie Davis Allen, otherwise known as Jacqueline D. Allen or Jackie Allen, grew up in the Cumberland Mountains of Appalachia. As the next eldest daughter of a coal miner father and a stay at home mother, she was the first in her family to attend and graduate from college. Her siblings, in their own right, are accomplished, though she is the only one, to date, that has discovered the gift of writing.

Graduating from Radford University, with a Bachelor's of Science degree in Early Education, she taught in both public and private schools. For over a decade she taught private art classes to children both in her home and at a local Art and Framing Shop where she also sold her original soft sculptured Victorian dolls and original christening gowns.

She resides in northern Virginia with her husband, taking much needed get-aways to their mountain home near the Blue Ridge Mountains, a place that evokes memories of days spent growing up in the Appalachian Mountains.

A lover of hats, she has worn many. Following marriage to her college sweetheart, and as wife, mother, grandmother, teacher, tutor, artist, writer, poet and crafter, she is a lover of art and antiques, surrounding herself, always, with books, seeking to learn more.

In 2015 she authored *Looking for Rainbows, Poetry, Prose and Art*, and in 2017, *Dark Side of the Moon*. Both books of mostly narrative poetry were published by Inner Child Press and were edited by hulya n. yilmaz in 2019, *No Illusions. Through the Looking Glass*, which was nominated to be considered for a Pulitzer Prize by the publisher and editor of Inner Child Press, ltd.

http://www.innerchildpress.com/jackie-davis-allen.php
jackiedavisallen.com

Adam Mickiewicz
1798-1855

Weary, exhausted, responsibilities on his mind,
A life to live, literary work to do, children,
And a wife not quite right in her mind.

Poet, activist, arrested, deported.
In despair, he thought of giving up.

The world, heavy on his shoulders,
A wife unable to cope, six children,
And cholera, about to swallow him up.

In the space, of less than a year,
Alas, both he and his wife passed away.

Considered as Poland's greatest poet,
Did his name, fame or acclaim,
Offer any consolation to his children?

An Autumn Song

fade the night
shine the light
drip drop the dawn

autumn sings
of coming days
of drifting banks of snow

of lives beginning to shiver
like little rowboats
with nowhere to go

Windstorm

The times are changing

And if there is a man, who
in the knowing
slips off of his best intentions,

and counts it but naught,

might not the audience
find him at fault
for trying to compete

with the windstorm,

that threatens
to shake him
off his pedestal?

What might one, then, think
of the spectators,
who are now expecting, demanding?

A refund for the price paid?

Tzemin Ition Tsai

Tzemin Ition Tsai

Dr. Tzemin Ition Tsai comes from the Republic of China (Taiwan). In addition to being a professor of literature at a university, he is more committed to writing poems, novels, and proses. He is also an editor of “Reading, Writing and Teaching” academic text, an International editor of "Contemporary dialogues" literary periodical in Macedonia, and Vice-Chairman of the International Jury of the SAHITTO INTERNATIONAL AWARD in Bangladesh, and a columnist for “Chinese Language Monthly” in Taiwan.

In a wide range of literary creations, he is particularly fond of interesting stories or novels, and writing articles or poems about the feelings of nature and human beings. He has won many national literary awards. His literary works have been anthologized and published in books, journals, and newspapers in more than 55 countries and have been translated into more than 24 languages.

Freedom

Beneath the heavens, vast and boundless stars,
Freedom whispers in the night,
Alone, I tread the path, my spirit scarred by war,
Yet still I stand, seeking that infinite light.

In the woods, where ancient silver leaves,
Embrace the land once free, now chained,
Each tree, each blade of grass now grieves,
For the silent earth, to sorrow's reign.

Within my heart, an eternal flame does burn,
Dreams of distant fields to which we belong,
The rivers sing, their pure and steadfast song,
As mist returns to shores where grasses yearn.

The peaks rise high, their icy light aglow,
Guarding the storm that rends the earth apart,
Yet freedom calls, through every valley's flow,
The nameless brave who fought, and did depart.

O thunder deep within the soul,
Heroes vanish at history's distant cry,
Echoes ring, yet spring's winds cease to roll,
Fear guides the land, where shadows clearly lie.

The Shepherd's Heart

Through storm and snow, the hills laid bare,
The shepherd treads alone, frost's chill in air.
What care has he for springtime long past?
His eyes, keen and clear, behold at last
The untamed road that leads him home,
A path of dreams where freedom roams.
The flock moves on, in dawn's embrace,
Knowing well where they find their place.
The skies stretch wide, serene and bright—
Is freedom waking in that light?
Or does eternal peace reside,
Unbroken still, by time's long tide?
The sheep, they follow without a thought,
Yet in his soul, deep battles fought—
To live for self, or in the glow
Of a distant star, that leads so slow.
He ponders life's winding road,
Its joys, its griefs, its gentle load.
And everywhere, both near and far,
Comfort and sorrow, twin-born are.
The mountains steep, the valleys wide,
His thoughts like rivers side by side.
Where truth and solid ground might be,
In whispered fates and destiny?
In quiet times, the sky turns gold,
And in its light, the wisdom old,
He feels, though still he walks alone,
Through fields where peace at last is known—
Found a way out, but it only cost nothing but a shepherd's heart.

Why Does That Star Follow Me from Afar?

I have long refused to ask
Why that star forever follows me from afar.
In the silent sky,
It gleams like a scar, so deeply marred.
Beneath its sorrowful light I tread,
Seeking witness to my endless night.
The paths I've walked, rugged and long,
Joy so fleeting, sorrow so strong.
Still, the star guards from its distant place,
Silent, watching fate's tides pass through shadows' trace.
Has it seen my pain?
Or does it carry silent mercy in its reign?
Though years may divide us still,
Maybe the star already knows what I don’t know,
Maybe the star has already found what I'm looking for.
And so, it shines, unchanged, distraught.
Yet I cannot forget, beneath the storm’s despair,
But I can't forget sinking into the dark night in the storm.

Shareef Abdur Rasheed

Shareef Abdur-Rasheed, AKA Zakir Flo was born and raised in Brooklyn, New York. His education includes Brooklyn College, Suffolk County Community College and Makkah, Saudi Arabia. He is a Veteran of the Viet Nam era, where in 1969 he reverted to his now reverently embraced Islamic Faith. He is very active in the Islamic community and beyond with his teachings, activism and his humanity.

Shareef's spiritual expression comes through the persona of "Zakir Flo" . Zakir is Arabic for "To remind". Never silent, Shareef Abdur-Rasheed is always dropping science, love, consciousness and signs of the time in rhyme.

Shareef is the Patriarch of the Abdur-Rasheed Family with 9 Children (6 Sons and 3 Daughters) and 41 Grandchildren (24 Boys and 17 Girls).

For more information about Shareef, visit his personal FaceBook Page at :

https://www.facebook.com/shareef.abdurrasheed1
https://zakirflo.wordpress.com

Mickiewicz

Adam Mickiewicz
B 1798 ~ D 1856

Amazing Polish master poet
his art concentrated on realism
mortality of all creation
especially mankind
life on earth designed to expire
though the habit of mankind is
to succumb to his/her appetite
be wealth. Power, glitter that is
attractive on the surface but
beyond that is worthless
in his piece: "Storm"
a ship at sea being torn to
pieces with men aboard
fighting to survive the violent
storm to no avail
would give anything to stay
alive at that defining moment
realize the true worth of the
glitter that puts mankind in a
mindless trance
he expressed that which has
no price tag because things
such as love, honesty, loyalty
truth, generosity
the priceless value of divine
god given qualities
the spirit moved him

So, What You Thankful For?

you got the right to gobble up
everything in sight
that you believe might makes right?
sooo what are you thankful for?
the prospect of getting mo, mo, mo?
peoples of earth would be thankful
if you were gone
like the innocent ones killed, maimed
by the drones you flown over their homes
plies of smoked rubble, flesh, bones
soo what you thankful for?
imposing unjust laws that suppress the hordes?
you who took god out the script cause you want
all mankind to call you lord incarnate
then have dem sing a song
with god bless you on it
say " heel lord master for your wars
wars fought to preserve our freedom at its core "
free to be brainwashed in lockstep,
robots controlled
by high tech,
void of free thinking, self-respect
who never should question your lies, hypocrisy,
steal from the peoples and call it democracy
dem should call ya'll " Dem a Crazzy '
soo what ya'll thankful for
that you're a fascist pimp with a stable of whores?
i'll tell ya what i'll be thankful for
when that day when you stand to be judged by
command in front of him who created all of them
men, women, jinn
and be paid the just wage that you earned
from beginning to end
on that day i wouldn't want to be you my friend

Breath..,

deeply let it out slowly,
vibe on the holy scribe
strive to know thee
clean the cranium
empty the mind of stress
don't think just relaxing
ride your flow
strive mellow, grow
derive direction go
easy
don't try pleasing
just be a light glow
treat the soulful yearning
to be free
leaves blowing on a tree
leaves me knowing thee
unseen but in full effect
the meaning of respect
life being living out the
purpose
oh mankind rehearse the verse
oh mankind reverse what's cursed
breathe deeply, let it out slowly
vibe on the holy name
closer then the jugular vein

Noreen Snyder

Noreen Ann Snyder has been writing since she was a teenager. She writes a variety of different topics. Her favorite poetic forms are Sonnets, Blitz, Haiku, Tanka, and Free Verse. She always learning different poetic forms.

Noreen Ann Snyder is a poet, writer, and an author of five books, (four books are co-authored with her late husband, Garry A. Snyder.) Her poetry is in several Inner Child Press Anthologies. She is the founder ofThe Poetry Club on Facebook.

Adam Mickiewicz's

He was a Poland poet, a writer,
and a political activist.
His poetic Epic, "Pan Tadeusm,"
was his masterpiece.
It's about love, honor, and patriotism.

He touched so many lives
not just through his poetry,
but also as a loving, caring human being.
He was patriotic, cared and loved his country
but he was deported from his country
never to return.

His poet friend, Krasinski, said this
after hearing about Mickiewicz's death,
"For men of my generation, he was milk and honey,
gall and descend from him.
He carried us off in the surging billow
of his inspiration and cast us into the world."

These Roses

These roses are still here
(not as many)
standing in the green vase,
droopy, dried, dead, and dark dark red
but they are still special to me.
My Teddy Bear Darling bought them for me
for our Anniversary
twenty plus years ago.
Who will take care of my flowers
when I'm gone?
Will they be thrown in the trash?
I pray not.

To Be a Winner

To be a winner
is to keep on trying
until you succeed
and never give up.

To be a winner
is to know that it's okay to make mistakes
and learn from them so you can avoid
it the next time.

To be a winner
is to have confidence in yourself
and what you do
but not to be egocentric.

To be a winner
is to be successful
without stepping on
anyone's toes.

To be a winner
is to know whatever you're victorious in
there will be someone out there
who's better than you.

To be a winner
is to be a good sport
whether you win or lose.

Elizabeth E. Castillo

Elizabeth Esguerra Castillo

Elizabeth Esguerra Castillo is a multi-awarded and an Internationally-Published Contemporary Author/Poet and a Professional Writer / Creative Writer / Feature Writer / Journalist / Travel Writer from the Philippines. She has 2 published books, "Seasons of Emotions" (UK) and "Inner Reflections of the Muse", (USA). Elizabeth is also a co-author to more than 60 international anthologies in the USA, Canada, UK, Romania, India. She is a Contributing Editor of Inner Child Magazine, USA and an Advisory Board Member of Reflection Magazine, an international literary magazine. She is a member of the American Authors Association (AAA) and PEN International.

Web links:

Facebook Fan Page

https://free.facebook.com/ElizabethEsguerraCastillo

Google Plus

https://plus.google.com/u/0/+ElizabethCastillo

The Slavic Bard

In a whispered lore of shadowed and harlequin nights,
Where dreams entwine with fading lights,
There stands a name, a voice of eclectic grace—
Adam Bernard, a timeless trace.
Born from the heart of Poland's soul,
A bard whose words could make one whole,
He walked the fields where history wept,
And in his verses, the passion leapt.
By Vistula's banks, his spirit soared high,
In tales of love and freedom poured devoid of sigh,
With each pen stroke, the hidden past ignites,
A symphony of hopes and wondrous plights.
Ode to the lost, the brave, the dainty free,
In every line, echoes of humanity,
With visions drawn from pipe dreams unspun,
In twilight's glow, his mighty battles won.
Through misty valleys, legendary icons born,
His poems like the dew and misty dawn,
For every heart that seeks to find,
A solace in the dark, so kind.
He weaves in history's golden thread,
The echoes of the undying great dead,
A voice that calls from ages long past,
In every heartbeat, a shadow was cast.
So let us raise our cups, sing our song,
To Adam Bernard, where we belong,
For in his words, we still await,
A world in harmony, a bond of fate.

Mystic Dreams

In the hush of night, where shadows weave,
Whispers of thine wonder entice us to really believe,
A mystic tapestry spun from the dreamy silken thread,
Of what lies beyond, where the restless dare tread.
Stars paint the blank canvas with an illumination that's fleeting,
Each twinkle's a promise, a heartbeat, a greeting,
In the realm of dreams, where the mundane fades,
Reality blurs, and the heart serenades.
Mountains of courage, valleys of grace,
Time bends, stands still, and bows to this mystical place,
We dance with the moon's rhythm, embrace the unknown,
In the cradle of deafening silence, we find our own throne.
Visions of infectious laughter, reflections of tears,
A mosaic of hopes, and the echo of fears,
With each whispered secret, the heart takes flight,
As dreams become wings in the stillness of the dark night.
Yet dawn's gentle light creeps in with a sigh,
Pulling us back to the world, oh so shy,
But we carry the magic, as daylight returns,
For dreams are the embers from which our heart burns.
So, hold to those visions, let them not fade my dear,
For in every heartbeat, a dream is relayed devoid of fear,
With courage to chase what the night softly brings,
We awaken our souls to the song that life sings.

The Empath

In the quiet hum of a bustling modern street,
Where voices blend and strangers meet,
There walks a soul armed with a tender heart,
An empath, playing an unseen part.

With thine eyes like windows, deep and wide,
They feel the world, and let it glide
Through fingertips, like melting snow,
Each joy and sorrow, they come to know.

They sense the cheer, a vibrant hue,
But also, the whispers of pain so true,
A heavy cloak of unspoken cries,
They carry silently, beneath the grey skies.
In crowded rooms where shadows loom,
They find the light, dispel the gloom,
With every smile, they weave a thread,
Connecting hearts, where words are left unsaid.
Yet in this Divine Gift, there's too much weight to bear,
A raging storm of feelings, too much to share,
For not all truths are light and free,
Some linger long, like a haunting melody.

But still, they stand with open hands,
To catch the dreams and broken plans,
An intricate dance of give and take,
A fragile balance, for kindness's sake.

So, here's to the empaths, the subtle guides,
Who walk among us like angels, where love abides,
May they find comfort in their own sweet ways,
And learn to shine through the cloudy days.

Mutawaf Shaheed

Mutawaf Shaheed

C. E. Shy has been writing since the seventh grade. He continued writing through high school, until he became more involved in sports. After his graduation, he worked at the White Motors Company where he wrote for the company's newspaper. He started a column called: "The Poet's Corner." That was his first published work.

www.innerchildpress.com/c-e-shy.php

Crossings . . . Adam Mickiewicz

Surrounded by borders he had
to cross just to make sense of it
all. Expressing himself to those
would hear.

Touching on themes familiar to some
Relating stories about somethings to
come. Balancing words on the tip of a
pen.

Touching lives with his sayings and verse.
Searching for meanings to share with the
world outside his door. Finding comfort in
world that he toured.

Enjoy

Pay special attention to the latest
rendition of the new edition of a
reworked plan of the same old stand.

Take the first letter of sentence
and color it red. The very next
word to it, put it second to last.

Change the title, then call it brand new.
Find another PhD, say he's the newest
Harvard grad.

Infer his credentials can't be challenged.
Tell them his dad was the first guy to play
the rhythm and blues, he taught
John Lee Hooker and Jimmy Reed too.

They are prepared to listen to things
that don't have any sound. Tell them
you are going to take all of them when
you go to Mars

Even though the rocket ship was only
built for ten. The others, tell them you'll
be back to get them a little later on.

They may ask what are they going to do
for water and clean air? Tell them you'll
send them some back from up there.

Remember not to mention any of this
information to the Negro, keep your eyes
on them until we send for you.

Delectable

Appetizer

5 dozen roach legs sautéed in mouse tears then lightly breaded with pig crud. Blue Jay intestines stuffed with maggot eggs. Rat feet with mashed mosquitoes' brains. Boil for 3 minutes in Lake Erie water. Then enjoy.

Salad

Blanched Poison Ivy leaves covered with aged oak bark. Baby grapefruit rinds in mustard plaster. Crushed spider webs added for crunchiness. Grilled baby lizard lungs marinated along with toad tongues to enhance the palate. Ape sweat for added flavor.

Entre'

Bar B Qued bat backs soaked in rubbing alcohol for 2 hours before putting on the grill. Fire up the grill with drift wood and abandoned houses and wood from the shores of Lake Huron. Rack of buzzard legs wrapped in dog hair. Hog pasta roasted in skunk skins. Char broiled monkey eyes incased in chitterlings flavored with moth butter.

Dessert

Chilled Devils food soup covered with moose scabs and lion musk.

hülya
n.
yılmaz

Of Turkish descent, hülya n. yılmaz [sic] is Professor Emerita (Penn State, U.S.A.), Director of Editing Services (Inner Child Press International, U.S.A.), and a trilingual literary translator. Before her poetry and prose publications, she authored an extensive research book in German on cross-cultural literary influences.

Her works of literature include a trilingual collection of poems, memoirs in verse, prose poetry, short stories, a bilingual poetry book, and two books of poetry (one, co-authored). Her poetic offerings appeared in numerous anthologies of global endeavors.

hülya writes creatively to attain and nourish a comprehensive awareness for and development of our humanity.

hülya n. yılmaz, a traveler on the journey called "life" . . .

Writing Web Site
https://hulyanyilmaz.com/

Editing Web Site
https://hulyasfreelancing.com

like an eagle*

İstanbul dons a large number of majestic forts

Those structures from many ancient histories
May today not appear as powerful anymore
But the debris alone suffice to astound
The willing eye through a mere peek
At the hauntingly mighty Bosphorus,
In sync with the influential breaths
That many civilizations of the past
Have generously left in it to last

I haven't been there in too long of a while
In an empirical sense, that is
Frequent visits of my fertile imagination
Have otherwise sated my hunger and thirst
My longing for the dead who were left behind
And all my cravings for the impeccable times
Have been re-lived, time and again, in harmony
Amid the scents of a caring love ever so painstakingly

I borrowed an eagle's eye on this special day
Then perched atop a bastion and began to sway

Palaces, teahouses, trolleys, Bazaars, Cafés, fishermen
Rare carpet-Kilim and antiquities-selling ambitious shops
Yachts, stately mosques, the famed Dolmabahçe Sarai
Freighters, speed-boats, Hovercrafts, scenic jogging paths
Do not interest me in the least . . . the eagle's eye is a loan
Of a refined delicacy. I refuse to waste it for the mundane

On the bottom of the Bosphorus, all of a sudden,
Underneath a recent undercurrent, oh so sullen!
Amid seagrass . . .

I spotted my brass keychain
Of four distinctive keys
On it, my elephant carried on

I towed it heroically
Its movable, pretty trunk
Waved at me ecstatically

I guided us all
To the astonishing Sinopian coasts
To my breathtakingly serene flat-sanctuary

But, I found, to my demise
It no longer was there

Only then, did i recall my dream of last year
On the night of the 2nd month's 14th

And . . .

My loaner eye wept

* "like an eagle" is an old poem, one that appeared in one of my published poetry books. While doing the research on Adam Mickiewicz, where he died in particular, I was immediately reminded of my elegiac verses here. I cannot think far enough back when I have been to Istanbul the last time. It is in that Turkish city where most of my deceased family members rest. Thus, within the context of Mickiewicz' life, I could relate to the frequent traveler role.

seeking national freedom

if

knowing that imprisonment is a high possibility,
that an exilic life could be one's sole livability,
that freedom anywhere would remain a dream
        not to ever come true,
but still staying wedded to activities geared toward
        that ideal
is

not the core trait of a determined traveler
on this journey we call "life,"

what else would that be?

a self-appointed pilgrim?

postmortemly claimed

appeals not ever allowed

no freedom at all

Teresa E. Gallion

Teresa E. Gallion was born in Shreveport, Louisiana and moved to Illinois at the age of 15. She completed her undergraduate training at the University of Illinois Chicago and received her master's degree in Psychology from Bowling Green State University in Ohio. She retired from New Mexico state government in 2012.

She moved to New Mexico in 1987. While writing sporadically for many years, in 1998 she started reading her work in the local Albuquerque poetry community. She has been a featured reader at local coffee houses, bookstores, art galleries, museums, libraries, Outpost Performance Space, the Route 66 Festival in 2001 and the State of Oklahoma's Poetry Festival in Cheyenne, Oklahoma in 2004. She occasionally hosts an open mic.

Teresa's work is published in numerous Journals and anthologies. She has two CDs: *On the Wings of the Wind* and *Poems from Chasing Light*. She has published three books: *Walking Sacred Ground, Contemplation in the High Desert* and *Chasing Light.*

Chasing Light was a finalist in the 2013 New Mexico/Arizona Book Awards.

The surreal high desert landscape and her personal spiritual journey influence the writing of this Albuquerque poet. When she is not writing, she is committed to hiking the enchanted landscapes of New Mexico. You may preview her work at

http://bit.ly/1aIVPNq or ***http://bit.ly/13IMLGh***

Mickiewicz Legacy

Polish bard, romantic dramatist, essayist
and political activist in the 19th century.
Literature tells us, you were a great poet.

That did not put bread on your table.
The ailments of poverty,
imprisonment and exile
did not stop your creative flow

Your legacy of the word
rides into the 21st century
on the wings of the highs and
lows of your life.

As One

When I look at you, I smile.
My knees bend in reverence
for love beneath the sunset
in the garden of bliss.

The taste of love
drips from your third eye.
Gives moisture to the sand.

Let us walk in the sacred wetness.
Feel beyond the body,
soothing the soul
in an ecstatic massage.

My smile grows bigger
as I remember,
the last time we walked as one.

Call of Autumn

I kiss the green goodbye.
Embrace my yellow radiance.
A last kiss to the sun.
I melt into the desert sand.

A return to earth written in time.
I spread my leaves across the ground
with gratitude and grace.

Another year of spiritual unfoldment
raises my consciousness
and tags my heart.

I hear the sound
of sandy love notes
inviting me to rest.

Ashok K. Bhargava

Ashok K. Bhargava

ASHOK BHARGAVA is a poet, writer, inspirational speaker and a literary consultant. He has attended poetry conferences in Italy, Turkey, India and Philippines. His latest book "Riding the Tide" about his battle with cancer has been translated and published in Arabic, Hindi, Telugu and Bengali languages. He is a contributing writer to several anthologies worldwide including World Poetry Almanac 2014. He has been published in numerous print and online magazines.

Ashok has won many accolades including Poet Ambassador to Japan, Kalidasa International award, World Poetry Lifetime Achievement award, Writers Beyond Borders Peace award and Tapsilog Leadership award for his community involvement. He is founder of Writers International Network Canada Society to discover, nourish, recognize and celebrate writers, poets and artists and to assist them to network with the community at large. He is the author of eight books of poetry and one anthology. He is Artist-in-Residence at Moberly Arts & Cultural Centre and also co-edits the literary section of The Link Newspaper.

Loss of Existence

perched on
edge of time
devastation
mushrooms
with bullets
and bombs

hiding
in the safety of bunkers
politicians
pretentiously
promise
to save us from the
of genocidal hatred
and endless
blood oozing
agony

unstoppable war
every iota on spin

grief becomes albatross
reviled
a prelude to
mystic
patriotism
whole generation
lost

Mix and Mingle

in the blood-stained soil
blooms
a flower then another and another.

they look at each other and around
and wonder about
the victims and the victimizers
oppressors and the oppressed
Jews and Arabs
Israelis and Palestinians
at the futility of hate.

flowers and trees
different roots
intermingle
in the same soil
same blood
in perfect harmony.

why can’t
the Jews and the Arabs?

Life is Suffering

I thought that the light will change it all, I would not be
so bitter of darkness, of the lonely nights,
of the things that you possess and I don't.

I thought it will help tame my raw desires,
not needing fulfilling and that at my age
a beautiful girl would not make me envious.

But here I am, incomplete—
When I see you, I still don't know how to resist
your magnetic pull.

Once again, I begin to write a poem
about light, blossoms and trees
and butterflies.

Life is suffering, Buddha taught. He's right.
Which brings more comfort
Not sure -
Abstaining or fulfilment.

Caroline 'Ceri Naz' Nazareno Gabis

Caroline 'Ceri' Nazareno-Gabis

Caroline 'Ceri Naz' Nazareno-Gabis, author of Velvet Passions of Calibrated Quarks, World Poetry Canada International Director to Philippines is a multi-awarded poet, editor, journalist, educator, peace and women's advocate. She believes that learning other's language and culture is a doorway to wisdom.

Among her poetic belts include **Gabrielle Galloni Memorial Panorama International Youth Award** 2022, Panorama Youth Literary Awards 2020, 7th Prize Winner in the 19th, 20th and 21st Italian Award of Literary Festival; Writers International Network-Canada ''Amazing Poet 2015'', The Frang Bardhi Literary Prize 2014 (Albania), Poet Journalist Award 2014 (Tuzla, Istanbul, Turkey) and World Poetry Empowered Poet 2013 (Vancouver, Canada). She's a featured member of Association of Women's Rights and Development (AWID), The Poetry Posse, Galaktika Poetike, Asia Pacific Writers and Translators (APWT), Axlepino and Anacbanua. Her poetry and children's stories have been featured in different anthologies and magazines worldwide.

Links to her works:

http://panitikan.ph/2018/03/30/caroline-nazareno-gabis/

https://apwriters.org/author/ceri_naz/

http://www.aveviajera.org/nacionesunidasdelasletras/id1181.html

Liberty's Flame

In every Polish heart,
Adam Mickiewicz's spirit is seared and loved,
The National poet was born,
His poetry was a voice
Revered as scholar, a patriot and hero,
His words flourished,
His tales of freedom woven by pen.
He spoke of liberty's blaze,
This bard awoken his homeland,
His words reside
In Poland's dawn.

Panacea of The Wind

Zypheria whispers
Through the lofty pines,
The sentinels stood on mountain tops,
The legendary cure,
Is a miraculous breeze,
That heals all wounds
Of treacherous storms and cyclones.
The crystal vial of a mythical wind,
Suffuse at every altitude,
Panacea grants eternal calmness,
The traveler's cloak flies to the clouds,
Windshield's potions and herbs infuse,
Healing nestles in beautiful minds,
The legendary care for perilous odyssey.

Inscrutable

My thoughts glide
Through the labyrinth
Seeking answers in quietude,
When shadows' face
The guardian moon,
Yet, all remains a mystery.
Questions scatter across the sky,
Each possibility lies in the stars,
Dreams and desires reach distant lands,
The voices of hopes and fears are elusive,
Unfathomable, buried deep,
Into the abyss of unsolved mazes,
I realize, these fleeting myths
Inscrutable challenges to be embraced.

Swapna Behera

Swapna Behera

Swapna Behera is a trilingual poet, translator, environmentalist, editor from India and author of seven books of different genres including one on children's literature on Environment. She is the recipient of International UGADI AWARD 2019, honoured from Gujurat Sahitya Akademi 2022, 2021 International Poesis Award of Honor as Jury, Pentasi B World Fellow Poet, Honoured Poet of India from Seychelles Government and International awards from Algeria, Morocco, Kajhakhstan, modern Arabic Literary Renaissance of Egypt, International Arts Council Argentina etc. Her stories, poems, articles are published in many International and National magazines and ezines. Her poem A NIGHT IN THE REFUGEE CAMP is translated into 67 languages. She has received over 60 National and International Awards. At present she is the Cultural Ambassador for India and South Asia of Inner Child and the life member of Odisha Environmental Society

Email
swapna.behera@gmail.com

Web Site
http://swapnabehera.in/

Adam Mickiewicz: the National Poet of Poland

who cares for the body?
"I have thrown off my body, spirit
I put on wings! "
says Adam Mickiewicz;
the national poet of Poland
romantic dramatist, publicist and political activist
you can stretch forth your hands even to the to the skies
you are the Master of your wish
you can weave rainbows of harmonies
you are immortal
the metaphors are as powerful as the storm
the lyrical intensity and episcopes
as calm as the sky
"I am the master
I am the master
me and my motherland are one"
as a Phoenix you are a revered figure
you say you are millions
the greater love from your heart reaches millions
your verses are journey of dots to existentialism
you are the lifelong apostle
of polish National freedom

two sides of my shadow

side 1

once upon a time
my shadow plundered
the depth, width and length
of my exuberant green existence
my verse rattled
nature twiddled in cobwebs
the shadow harrowed
piercing the subtle mirror

side 2

my shadow dances on debris or decks
on hilly hamlets or lagoons
swings like a sapling
dignity lies not in the body
at the end of the day a feeling
a queen being coronated

death is a bureaucrat

death speaks of confused collapses
isn't death a bureaucrat?
death writes wreath of roses
carrying the files of blind Karma
death is a yogi
omnipresent
yet, combination of invisible alphabets
death stumbles
enchants mantra as a hermit
all of a sudden death sparkle
with its multilayer identity
life's metamorphosis
celebrates death on the wings of a butterfly
the caterpillar sings
and silence echoes
eternal fragrance spreads
to sow seeds of lyrical harvest
in the cage of the chest

Albert 'Infinite' Carrasco

Albert 'Infinite' Carassco

Albert "Infinite The Poet" Carrasco is an urban poet, mentor and public speaker.

Albert believes his experience of growing up in poverty, dealing with drugs and witnessing murder over and over were lessons learnt, in order to gain knowledge to teach. Albert's harsh reality and honesty is a powerfully packed punch delivered through rhyme. Infinite grew up in the east part of the Bronx and still resides there, so he knows many young men will follow the same dark path he followed looking for change. The life of crime should never be an option to being poor but it is, very often.

Infinite poetry @lulu.com

Alcarrasco2 on YouTube

Infinite the poet on reverbnation

Infinite Poetry

www.lulu.com/us/en/shop/al-infinite-carrasco/infinite-poetry/paperback/product-21040240.html

www.innerchildpress.com/albert-carrasco

Adam Mickiewicz

I am a polish poet born in the Russian empire,
My passion for literature helped me create a new kind of romantic drama,
I put passion love and affection, history and culture mixed in poetic stanzas.
Politically active I also wrote about how being free the Russian empire,
I wanted to actually live how I imagined I'd live.
My fellow Philomaths were striving to make that accomplishment,
but the authorities arrested me and sent me to central Russia as punishment.
I continued to write.
Nothing was going to stop my passion, not even incarceration.
I've became a household name.
I have brought attention to polish poetry by never letting go of the reins,
as I strove for acknowledgment, and by doing so I gained fame.
My heart and art was with and for Poland,
but it reached all over and largely influenced Ukrainian literature.
I traveled the world teaching and preaching my beliefs,
the last days I spent on earth went on fight for freedom, for Poland.
I am the prolific writer and trail blazer … Adam Mickiewicz

Consequences

Numb fingers, sweaty du rag and wife beater, wore masks so that raw didn't get airborne like the virus and fuck with my sinuses. Hangers, soda and water to whip up a banger. Slabs and fresh gems to size up and ration orders. Look outs steerers and pitchers. Bosses, managers and gunners. This was the inner city system to battle oppression. All we had was the game and the streets. Cop, chef, bag, sell and repeat while trying to avoid human slabs and white sheets.

Violence came along with fast money, monopolizing in the hood with stamped and trademarked color goods made that fast money real bloody, whether you was attacking or defending guns were bust daily, when the smoked cleared mothers lived out their worse fear as they cradled their lifeless children screaming out... no not my baby. I have a lot of weight on my shoulders, I was my brothers keeper, got jacked by the reaper and became my brothers pallbearer. We wanted to live but it was live where we lived so some became angels before they could really spread their wings. I stood at besides holding vigils, when they didn't come thru I prayed to my crew... sorry homie, y'all know me, if I was there i would've saved you. Going to wakes was something i never wanted to get use too, but I did, Ortiz, Porta Coeli and montera been last viewing funeral homes since I was a kid.

Rain

Making it rain was our lifestyle, we was celebrating the cross over to wealth from poverty daily. Money was coming in faster than we could spent it so we went on spontaneous splurging sprees. A few stacks here, hundreds there, we had no cares throwing it in the air. In them whips we sat low low, in the bricks we blew choco chased by momo yelln out red, followed by Bellaco, for promo. "We got it good was the sales pitch". toothpaste and toothbrushes cleaned chains and rings to give it that extra bling, safes were full of Cha-Ching, we was hood rich fuckn with that white bitch. We dealt with the elements to stack dead presidents, winter, spring, summer and fall we was out there in housing developments. There was a lot of us, we wasn't a gang but we'll bang for each other and for that in god we trust. If everything went according to plan we would've been rich together living in estates built on owned land, we would've been crossing culdesacs in robes with a half a million on the pinky, wrist and in lobes to meet the mail man. We would've been driving exotics, flying in privates, doing business with people that have differently accents and dialects in different times zones and climates, if that knife wasn't thrusted and those guns would've jammed.

Michelle Joan Barulich

Michelle Joan Barulich

Michelle Joan Barulich was born in Honolulu, Hawaii on the island of Oahu. She started writing poetry and songs with her younger brother Paul. They have written many songs in their teen years. She is currently studying Alternative Medicine and would like to become a Homeopathic Doctor. Michelle loves all kinds of animals and birds; she does wild rehabilitation. She has also rescued rock pigeons that make great pets.

https://www.facebook.com/michelle.barulich

The Poet from Poland

Adam Mickiewicz is regarded as a national poet in Poland
Adam was a poet, publicist and a political activist
He is considered one of the greatest Slavic and European poets
Adam was also known as an activist striving for
Independence for Poland
In 1838 he became a Professor of Latin Literature
He had been written about and had many works
Dedicated to him by many authors
He was a respected person
All across the globe.

If you Stay

If you stay
I'll be complete
There's no time to weep from one's eyes
If you come, don't say goodbye
If you love me, don't turn around
Promise solid ground
Then your love will be found
If you stay
Love will be true
Come in from the rain
And I will love you
Keep your heart in my hands
It will return from empty lands.

The Emeralds

The liquid of life
Leaves you to bleed
Like a violin
There're four strings to the melody
The emerald of life is here and now
Do the best that you can do
Take a part in the circle
You will be counted for
Life is a gift
And a mystery too
Hold it in your hands
Try to solve the riddle of time
It takes us all for a ride.

Eliza Segiet

Eliza Segiet

Eliza Segiet graduated with a Master's Degree in Philosophy at Jagiellonian University.

Received *Global Literature Guardian Award* – from Motivational Strips, World Nations Writers Union and Union Hispanomundial De Escritores (UHE) 2018.

Nominated for the Pushcart Prize 2019, 2021.

Laureate *Naji Naaman Literary Prize 2020*,

International Award Paragon of Hope (2020),

World Award 2020 *Cesar Vallejo* for Literary Excellence. Laureate of the Special Jury *Sahitto International Award* 2021, World Award *Premiul Fănuș Neagu* 2021.

Finalist *Golden Aster Book* World Literary Prize 2020, *Mili Dueli* 2022, Voci nel deserto 2022.

At the international Festival of Poetry CAMPIONATO MONDIALE DI POESIA (2021/2022) she won the title of vice-champion of the world.

Award BHARAT RATNA RABINDRANATH TAGORE INTERNATIONAL AWARD (2022).

Award - *World Poets Association* (2023).

Laureate Between words and infinity *"International Literary Award (2023).*

The Destiny of the World

*In memory of Adam Mickiewicz**

He could feel the world
more, more strongly, differently...
He could foresee.
The History of the Future
was to complement his works.

It could have been so. Only if he had not listened to
the whispers of a certain count
who feared
that his work
might do harm...

That was sufficient. He decided!
The fire consumed most
of the foreseen, written down future.

Something remained, however.
From the letters to his friends
and fragments of the manuscript
lure traces of the world's fate,
which one day was to emerge from non-existence.

Unfortunately,
there aren't enough words to express
the prophetic vision of the
one who proclaimed:
*Call me not a critic, but a bard***.

He was right.
His contemporaries knew it
and so do those living today.

**Adam Bernard Mickiewicz (24th December 1798 – 26th November 1855) was a Polish poet, playwright, essayist, translator and political activist. He is celebrated as a national poet in Poland, Lithuania, and Belarus and recognized as a leading figure in Polish Romanticism. Among the "three bards," he is widely acknowledged as the greatest Polish poet.*

*** On the 3rd of May 1842, Mickiewicz said, "Do not call me a critic, but a bard" during a meeting at the Polish Literary Society.*

Translated by Dorota Stępińska

Dance

Her eyes said that
she wants to dance,
have fun, go crazy.

Perhaps
she envied others –
of their dancing feet.

She envelops in infirmity –
she cried.

Nobody saw her tears,
nobody saw that
like others
she craves for life.

Maybe he did not want to see?

Translated by Artur Komoter

Romeo

On the boundless ocean of love,
where the nightingales sang at dawn,
still you can hear voiceless words,
ineffable thoughts.

Silence, quiet,
which for centuries pulsate
and the frayed mark on the monument.
On the boundless ocean of the world
– the remaining feeling.
Maybe somewhere,
at a crossroad,
where the leaves tremble alone
the longed for Romeo
– is still waiting.

Translated by Artur Komoter

William S. Peters Sr.

Bill's writing career spans a period of well over 50 years. Being first Published in 1972, Bill has since went on to Author in excess of 50+ additional Volumes of Poetry, Short Stories, etc., expressing his thoughts on matters of the Heart, Spirit, Consciousness and Humanity. His primary focus is that of Love, Peace and Understanding!

Bill says . . .

I have always likened Life to that of a Garden. So, for me, Life is simply about the Seeds we Sow and Nourish. All things we "Think and Do", will "Be" Cause and eventually manifest itself to being an "Effect" within our own personal "Existences" and "Experiences" . . . whether it be Fruit, Flowers, Weeds or Barren Landscapes! Bill highly regards the Fruits of his Labor and wishes that everyone would thus go on to plant "Lovely" Seeds on "Good Ground" in their own Gardens of Life!

to connect with Bill, he is all things Inner Child

www.iaminnerchild.com

Personal Web Site

www.iamjustbill.com

In Remembrance for you Adam

I am the romantic,
I am the poet,
I am the one
Who hears the voices . . .
The voices screaming to be heard,
The voices of the downtrodden,
The voices within me
Fighting amongst themselves
For prevalence

My wonder leads me
To wander,
And doing so
I collect
Gems and treasures
To share with those
Who are thirsty
Those who hunger

I have communed with
The Sovereign,
The Royals,
The waif,
The vagrant,
The poor

I have wandered in the meadows
Along the shores of the great waters,
Atop the mountains,
And along the valleys,
And everywhere I turn,
Everywhere I look,
I listen . . . . and
I am greeted by those voices

Calling my name . . . ADAM

Peace

I did not think about it much
During the days of my youth,
But as I grew older,
I slowly began to realize
That though this world
Had its small pleasures
Joys, comforts, rewards,
And treasures
It was not the idyllic place
Of my desires,
My dreams,
My hopes,
Nor my needs

One does not have
To look hard
To see the overt
Hate, bias and indifference
That prevails itself upon us

Human life has grown to be
A statistic of insignificance
And it would appear
That our self-centered motives
Are all that matter
When we paint our soul- homes
With vibrant colors
To hide the uglines
That lives and breathes
Beneath the surface
Of our projected peace

We struggle amongst each other,
As well as within ourselves
In our attempts to find
An elusive solace
As we delude ourselves
Subversively embracing the chaos
Calling it Peace

We long within the depths of our Souls
To once again sit in the presence
Of our birthright ..... peace
And LOVE

And i

I speak often
To my ancestors
And other loved ones
Whom I have lost

I too hope
That when my moment
Of reconciliation arrives
I will be able to cross
That bridge made of rainbows
And once again embrace
The objects of my
Fathomless love

I have hopes
For this life
And the next
That my soul will find balance
Between the 'in' and 'ex' trinsic expressions
Of my existence

Memories flood my reason
And in spite of myself,
The longing consumes me,
And still I will not yeild
Or fully submit

What is this tryst
I have between fiction and fact
That plays its mesmerizing music
That drunkens my resolve

And has me fractally accepting
Kaleidoscopic reasoning
As a verity?

The deeper I dig
The more I realize
My shallowness
And the futility
Of my self-proclaimed
Understanding

I somehow realized
That not all open doors
Were meant to be entered
Nor exited,
Now are all windows
Meant to be opened

There is a light that
Sneaks through
The closed blinds
That affirms that
There is a Sun,
There is a Moon,
And they each have
Their purpose
.....
Me, i am upon my knees
Scratching in the dirt
In the darkness
Seeking immutable treasures
Hoping to clone my higher self
And bind it with some permanence
To my ultimate expectations

As to why I am here,
And to what end
Does this journey proceed

I honor each and every footstep
I have taken up to my 'Here',
And 'Now'
I acknowledge the
Power of Fate and Destiny
Contrived or not
And I.....

Opening Soon for Submissions

Stay Tuned

Messages

Poetry & prose

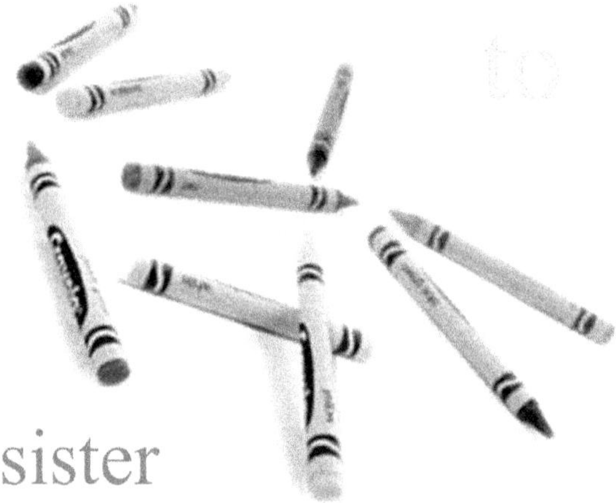

to

my sister

my daughter

my partner

my friend

Women of the Ink

October

2024

Featured Poets

~ * ~

Deepak Kumar Dey

Shallal 'Anouz

Adnan Al-Sayegh

Taghrid Bou Merhi

i
Fly
because
I Can
. . . said the Dreamer to the world.
www.iamjustbill.com

Deepak Kumar Dey

Deepak Kumar Dey, son of late Dr. G. C. Dey and Late Surama Dey, hails from Bagdia, Angul district of Odisha, is an ardent lover of nature and avid worshipper of poetry. He was a student of chemical engineering but passion of poetry attracted him to search divine bliss in nature. Since he has crossed many ordeals in his life and hazardous brusqueness yet he finds supreme God's benevolent presence and prudence. He never looks for social status or recognition. Through soulfulness he seeks Almighty's abundant grace and mercies. In arrayed words he weaves the magic of mirthful munificence and glory of God. […]

Description Of a Brief Moment

Tick-tick goes the clock, jeering sign comes up;
How discordant I am only for worldly measure,
Driven by deleterious passion, for now and after,
Zest for such a life in broad daylight puffs up.

Each step ruminates to rustle on dimming street,
Picking up my senses abysmally with no dalliance,
Tenderly I fall in love with delicate fragrance,
At my stimulus brows dreams bedazzle bright.

Like awakening birds sing when breeze suffuses,
Without hesitation for interminably mystical ecstasy-
Solely I adore, admire transcendental tendency;
On rosy canopy cupidity and succulence amazes.

Through casement this reminds sun in the east,
Pretending to myself I do revamp through mist.

Tragic Death...

What a horrible illusion from tragic distance!
When a reflective thought of pure delight-
Unnoticeably leaves its reduced chance,
Conventional notes can not get to its height.

Inevitable strivings are encapsulated by tempest,
A fateful beckoning in quest is trackless
When the thunderstorms cast the hardest,
The embodied purification turns out fateless.

The stroke of destiny is really so unbearable,
It's hitting hard punching the unseen marks.
Resolved contentment finds engulfing whirlpool,
Untimely, a cyclonic storm is sure to embark.

Blossoming flower, superseded by unkind touch,
Moans seeing uprooted trees' endangered approach.

Fateless

Black clouds are covering my sheltering sky, I see.
I can imagine a bolt of blue-thunderstorm will hit here-
To bother me, I cannot tell how hazardous it would be.
Let me bear it all alone and watch what comes to be.

I feel, I can inhale the hurting that I can not deny,
Never ever; do not think that I am too cowardly to stay.
Oh, yes! you can not see me in rain how much I cry.
Perhaps, it is my fate and has come out for longest stay.

No one can see the flowing flooding tears from my eyes,
Why you are beforehand? ask me not how I am able to hide.
It cannot or can heal me I know; you do not seem to mind.
I am determined not to sigh making louder cries.
Let my sufferings and sorrows go away or stay, nothing is in my mind.

Let me say the genuine told words of mighty minds, the wise;
"Have you seen, does a trusted wolf in sheep's guise pay the price?"
Forgive me, I beg your pardon, for I will not hide.
I will quietly bear grieving through my silent cries alongside.
Even if I am on the right side, wounds of your words cut deeply inside.

Oh, yes! for betterment, accepted the toughest lesson of life,

Do not try to lampoon and laugh mockingly when I choose to smile.
Forgive me, forgive me I beg you, I am kneading to smile a lot,
Let me continue in my stride, I was taught that revenge is not to be sought.

Shallal Anouz

Shallal 'Anouz is an Iraqi poet born in 1950, member: Union of Writers and Authors, he published six colocations of poetry and one novel, some of his works have been translated into English, Kurdish, French, and Italian. Around 25 books, letters, and dissertations have been written about his literary and creative career.

Trees of Hope

He once told me:
Don't suppress the joy that comes with tears,
Don't block the windows of dreams.
He once told me
To open the doors of happiness to the dawn,
Offer the warm antidote of hearts to those passing through hardship.
Wear the robe of those running towards the sun,
Hold on to the necklace of light that leads you to the peak of the day,
To be able to see
the destinies in their nakedness.
So, think not of going back.
Cling to the tree of hope at the height of your wound.
Set out off from the wail of pain and disappointment,
Cross the obstacles of setback.
Start running towards the end even if your legs fail you,
For the fast and deliberate steps
Always lead to the destination shore.
Why, whenever we say we have arrived, does the noise scold us?
And our roads are burdened with the rags of those who did not cross the river naked.
They left behind only the hooves of their horses
And exhausted donkeys
That were carrying the luggage of consolation to the other side of the dream.
I saw him again at the edge of perdition,
The space was vast,

Stretching out empty of the homeland's cries.
But the winds were pointing to the ends,
And the trees were rustling, provoking the birds.
And a hundred journeys away,
There was a wedding procession coming.

Translated into English by: Hussein Nasser jabr

Cities of Aridity

He sighs his sorrows late at night,
With a heavy grip of sleeplessness,
He bears the burden of his grief,
Weeping with tears for his stolen dream.
No one shares his mournful cries,
No one hears his anguished sighs.
All have gone, he stands alone,
Praying on the path of hope unknown.
He waits for the rain to fall,
To wash away the drought and all.

Translated into English by: Hussein Nasser jabr

A Soul Unmoored

On the bench of tragedies,
He sat, weary and forlorn,
Drowning in his sorrows,
Words barely escaping his lips.
He breathed the sighs of exile,
Lost and bewildered,
Cursing his wretched fate,
In the ears of the arrogant wind.
The place was crowded
With the recklessness of nomads
And the smoke of superstitions,
No distinction between
The headband of Sedition
And the rosary of Deception
But the homeland remained a child,
On the strings of his patience,
Carrying the rock of Sisyphus,
Waiting for the appearance of Janus.
And I have no business
With what the aftermath of the ordeal will lead to.
August 27, 2023
Janus: The god of hope in Greek mythology

Translated into English by: Hussein Nasser jabr

Adnan Al-Sayegh

Adnan Al-Sayegh (1955 Iraq), He left his homeland in 1993 and since 2004 lives in London. He has published 12 books, including Uruk's Anthem & The Dice Of The Text. He has received several international awards and has been invited to read his poems in many festivals across the world.

Pages From the Biography of An Exile - (6)

I'll kick my socks toward the sky
in solidarity with those who don't have shoes
and I'll walk barefoot
feeling the muds of the streets under my feet
staring at the faces of the glutted inside their
glass offices, O …
if human intestines were glass
so we could see how much they've stolen our bread,
O Lord
if You couldn't fill this starving stomach
where worms squirm & belch
why did you create me with these wolfing molars
And if You didn't flesh my bed with a twig-tender body
then why did You give me such burning arms
And if You didn't grant me a country to be safe in
why did You godsend my wandering feet
And if You became exasperated by my complaints
then why did You give me this mouth
gushed with screams night & day

Translated by Stephen Watts and Marga Burgui-Artajo

Extracts from The Dice of The Text

Why do we enhance history, while it is blunt and blind?
Why do we shine the words while they are in excess of days?
and of need.
Why does the inkwell hem, and there is a lot of ink in the blood?
....

We are who crushed by history
our days are ready to kneel
and also, our hands to clap and to be chained
and our revolutions have only brought us to the gallows.
....

I tell my fantasies to passersby,
to my right are the Ziggurats,
to my left is Abu Ghraib prison.
....

We fill our lungs with air. . .
our air which was stolen from the breath of the slain,
as if our life cycle is a distance between two gasps
and we can prolong it by embezzlements or by sighs.
....

as if paper is a mirror of the imagination
as if the text is our menstruating dreams
as if our exhalation is a digging in the air.
I pull 'and' from the language crib
and spread it in anyway
to pull me to my scattered meaning

under the book hooves,
and the boots
　　　which
　　　crossed our history in reverse;

Translated by Dr. Jenny Lewis and Amani Alabdily

Second Song to Inanna/Ishtar

Trains, histories, armies, and kisses have marched by.
Trees, wars and exiles have marched by.
Al Sayyab and Edith Sitwell have marched by –

while we stand on Embankment bridge musing about the murmurings of the
Tigris and the Thames –
two parallel histories that can neither meet nor part
and so leave us regretting what each has lost by the other's absence.

Oh generous Tigris!
Sweet Thames, run softly,
till I end my song...

…the sound of jazz from a homeless girl rises from under the bridge
and we dance along with the night to her music

until orange blossom flowers between our fingers
and the columns of the bridge, the roads, the shops, the pages grow green
as far as Walt Whitman.

When we surface we find our boat is rudderless –
not even Uta-napishtim can steer a drunken boat…
Oh Inanna, how do we get back to Uruk, destroyed by the flood?

We are washed from depths to depths,
passing river bank after river bank.

We didn't know that exile would go on so long,
that our journey would only bring loss.

So come close, let poetry be our country,
love, the flute and wine... how beautiful these countries are,
how creative, how expansive.

Translated by Jenny Lewis and Ruba Abughaida

Taghrid Bou Merhi

Taghrid Bou Merhi is a Lebanese multilingual poet, writer, journalist and translator. She has authored 21 books and translated 24 books to date, a presenter of 25 books.She is an active member of various literary and creative platforms and editor of 8 Magazine Arabic. She is an advisory member among ten internacional poetry consultants chosen by Chinese media giant CCTV.Lebanese ambassador in the International Fellowship for Creativity and Humanities, England-London. Her writings are part of several national and international magazines, newspapers, journals and anthologies. She has won many awards for her write-ups.

TAGHRID BOU MERHI
(Foz Do Iguaçu, Paraná, Brasil)
taghrid240@gmail.com

Little Girl

Inside me, there is a restless little girl

She left behind the echoes of a memory

Filled with the sleep of bitter wine
And scattered poems exhausted by insomnia

Her hearing became delicate
As her faded stories melted into wrinkles of silence

They dissolved among the depths of time
And collided upon the wreckage of her heart like a slamming door

What if you were a vibrant cry
And my throat was a flute that played the music of the soul?

We would gather honey from bees and ride on bird's wings

Take me with gentle care in a coffin
When we grow tired and darkness falls between us
Who will heal the wounds of wanderers and dreamers?

The wound is deep, and memories bleed on death's bed

How can I convince containers that the sound of intestines is just an argument amidst the crowd?

How can I peel away the trunk of questioning
When mirages are fabricated images that only know madness?

And when voices of confusion expand
Who will chase away the howling wolves moody winds,
and hungry ones?

The night has draped itself in its cloak

And you are the prophetess, and your heart is youthful
So walk among the clouds

Video Call!

Perhaps it was empty, that sad tone slipping through the crack of memory...

Often I would chase away the loneliness with a kiss into the air
and a smile and laughter, pretending joy...

The soul sought like a migrant, murmuring longing for an embrace that would be sustenance for eternity
But my grip would spoil the fibers of the heart
and permit resignation until the last breath

The failure for a meteor to fall from the sky
weighed heavily on me
And her voice, my mather
A prayer, conquered the repugnant distances

What congestion here in the details of video calls
My hands grew tired of waiting
and the voice dug into regrets
And I, not mastering the art of screaming...

If only I were

If only I were skilled in acting
or simulating longing with indifference
Before her eighty-year-old face, my desire to kiss her through the screen would expose
my weakness and lack of cunning

And often I failed to console myself before her calls and
when I offered a soul to gaze upon the face of my beloved

But I failed
and I don't think you realized

I would perform ablution after every call
I would wrap my arms, filled with longing and yearning,
around myself as solace for an embrace

I would pour out pain onto farewell letters
and I would weave a thread with God that hope never
breaks!!

Identity!

Your concept of tradition takes the form of behavior

It becomes your obsession to adhere to an identity that is not suited to your environment, religion, and culture.

When you perform rituals of blind imitation,
You conjure in your imagination interpretation and imbue it with the superficiality that satisfies your modern desires.

What you feel as evolution and civilization,
It's a dual level between rapid transition and general indicators.

And as you are a part of everything
The individual aspect intertwines with the collective aspect
Together forming a socially debatable model.

In every stage of life, there are different origins and growing intersections

So choose what suits you
And your individual and social levels.

To shed your skin and wear the skins of others

Is like a sacrificial altar that takes away everything you've been brought up on and acquired over the years.

Affirming identity has a hierarchical status

So choose your identity

And don't just be an obsession that only knows imitation.

Remembering

our fallen soldiers of verse

Janet Perkins Caldwell

February 14, 1959 ~ September 20, 2016

Alan W. Jankowski

16 March 1961 ~ 10 March 2017

The Butterfly Effect

"IS" in effect

Inner Child Press

News

Published Books

by

Poetry Posse Members

We are so excited to share and announce a few of the current books, as well as the new and upcoming books of some of our Poetry Posse authors.

On the following pages we present to you ...

Alicja Maria Kuberska

Jackie Davis Allen

Gail Weston Shazor

hülya n. yılmaz

Nizar Sartawi

Elizabeth E. Castillo

Faleeha Hassan

Fahredin Shehu

Kimberly Burnham

Caroline 'Ceri' Nazareno

Eliza Segiet

Teresa E. Gallion

Mutawaf Shaheed

William S. Peters, Sr.

Now Available

www.innerchildpress.com

Now Available

www.innerchildpress.com

Now Available

www.innerchildpress.com

Now Available

www.innerchildpress.com

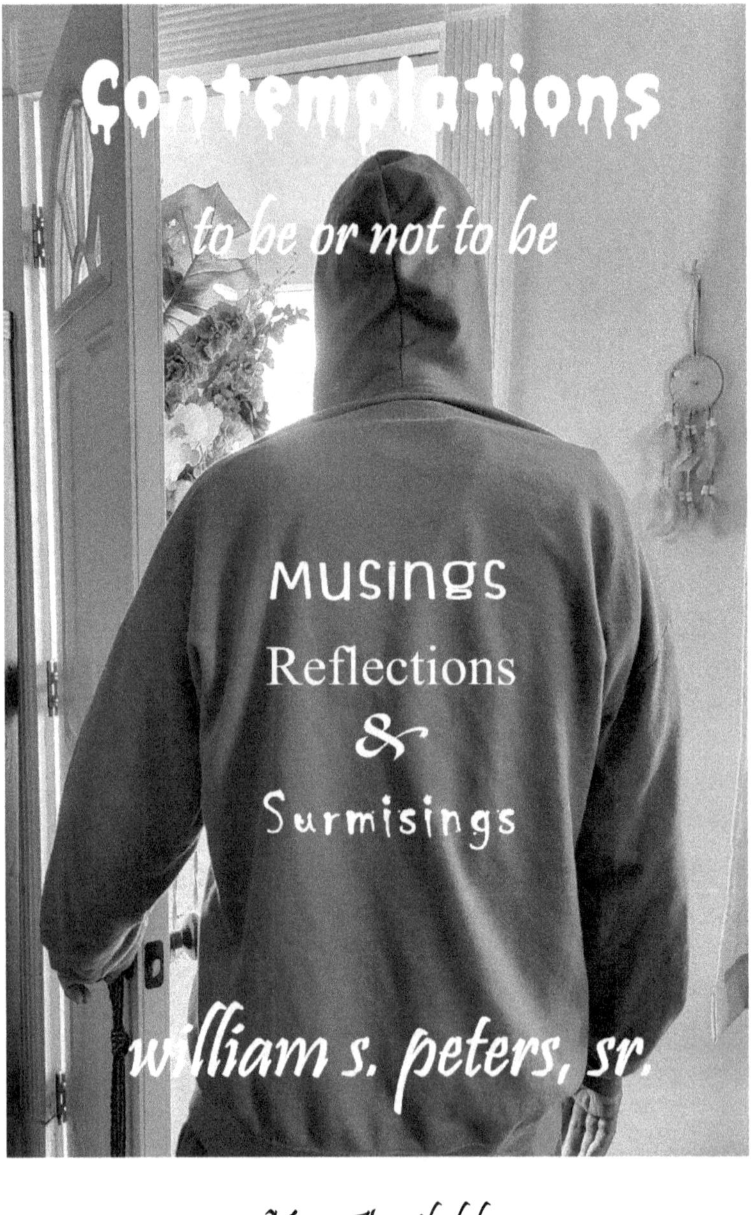

Now Available

www.innerchildpress.com

Now Available

www.innerchildpress.com

Once upon a Time
in
Turkey
hülya n. yılmaz

Now Available

www.innerchildpress.com

Now Available

www.innerchildpress.com

Now Available

www.innerchildpress.com

After the Frost
Alicja Maria Kuberska

Now Available

www.innerchildpress.com

Now Available at

www.innerchildpress.com

Now Available at

www.amazon.com/gp/product/B08MYL5B7S/ref=dbs_a_def_rwt_hsch_vapi_tkin_p1_i2

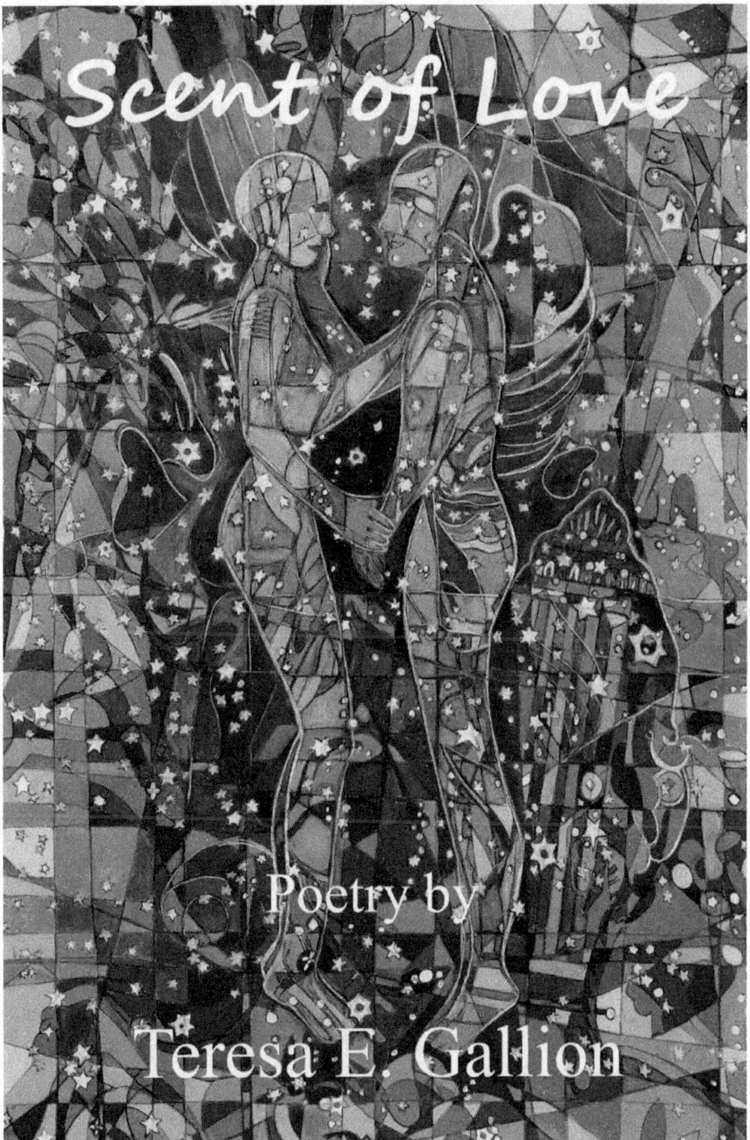

Now Available

www.innerchildpress.com

Now Available

www.innerchildpress.com

Now Available

www.innerchildpress.com

Now Available

www.innerchildpress.com

Now Available

www.innerchildpress.com

The Book of krisar
volume v
william s. peters, sr.

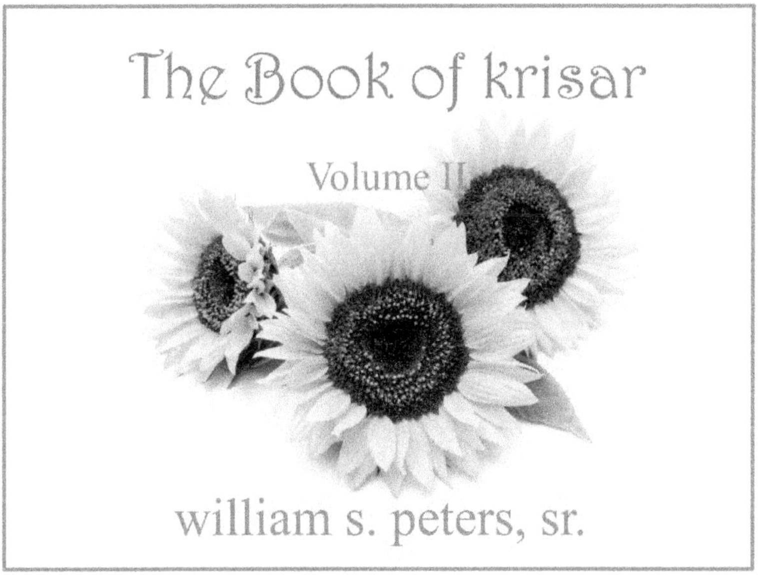

Now Available

www.innerchildpress.com

Now Available

www.innerchildpress.com

Now Available

www.innerchildpress.com

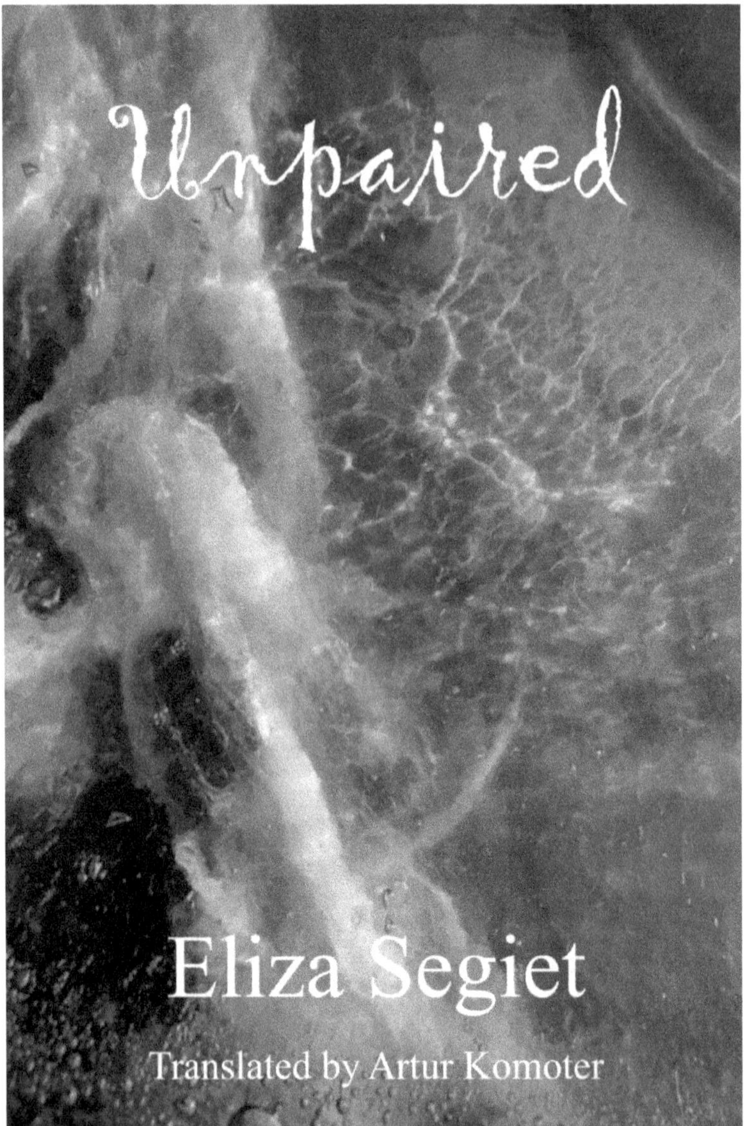

Private Issue

www.innerchildpress.com

Now Available

www.innerchildpress.com

Now Available at

www.innerchildpress.com

No Illusions
Through the Looking Glass
Jackie Davis Allen

this and that
a hodge-podge of hülya's … poetry
hülya n. yılmaz

Now Available at

www.innerchildpress.com

Now Available at

www.innerchildpress.com

Now Available at

www.innerchildpress.com

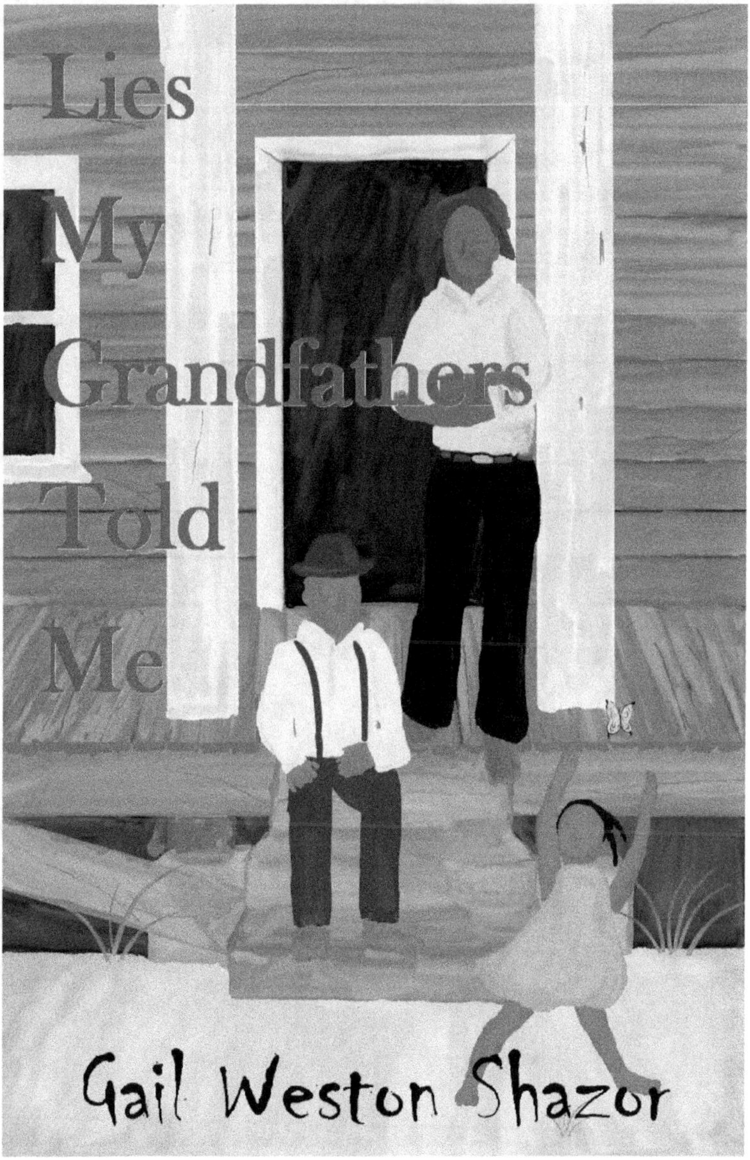

Now Available at

www.innerchildpress.com

Now Available at

www.innerchildpress.com

Mass Graves
Faleeha Hassan

Now Available at

www.innerchildpress.com

7 Days
in
Palestine
william s. peters sr.

Now Available at

www.innerchildpress.com

Now Available at

www.innerchildpress.com

my inner garden
~ expressions and discoveries ~
by
William S. Peters, Sr.

Other

Anthological

works from

Inner Child Press International

www.innerchildpress.com

Now Available

www.worldhealingworldpeacepoetry.com

Now Available

www.worldhealingworldpeacepoetry.com

Now Available

www.worldhealingworldpeacepoetry.com

Now Available

www.worldhealingworldpeacepoetry.com

Now Available

www.innerchildpress.com

Corona
Social Distancing
Poets for Humanity

Poetry
from the
Balkans
The Balkan Poets

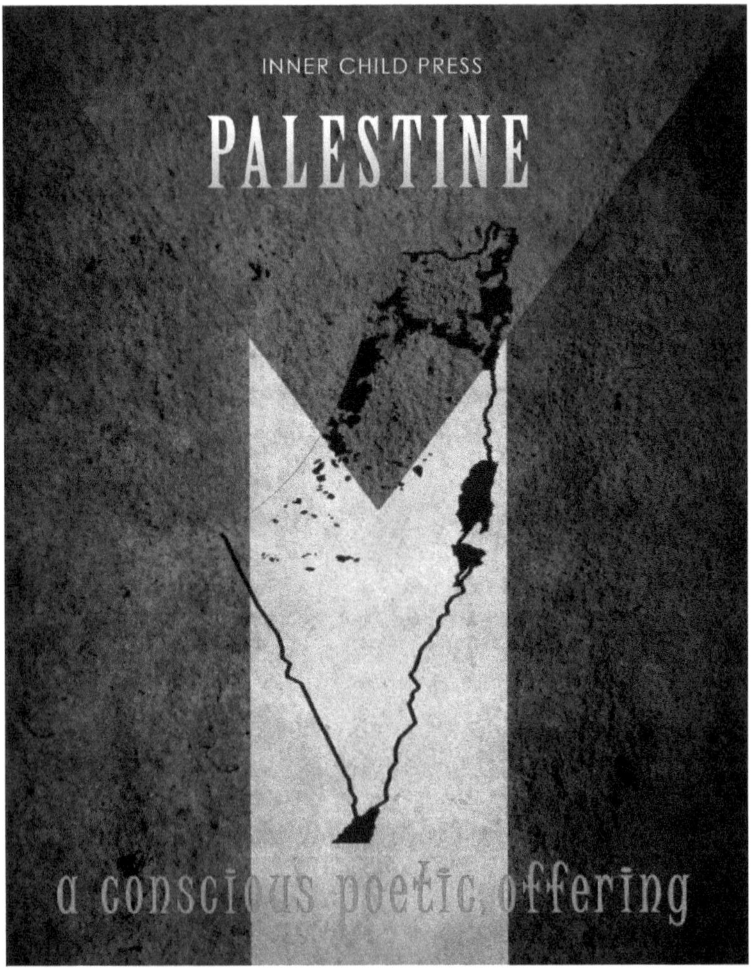
INNER CHILD PRESS
PALESTINE
a conscious poetic offering

INNER CHILD PRESS
WORLD HEALING
WORLD PEACE
2018
A Poetry Anthology for Humanity

Now Available

www.worldhealingworldpeacepoetry.com

Now Available

www.worldhealingworldpeacepoetry.com

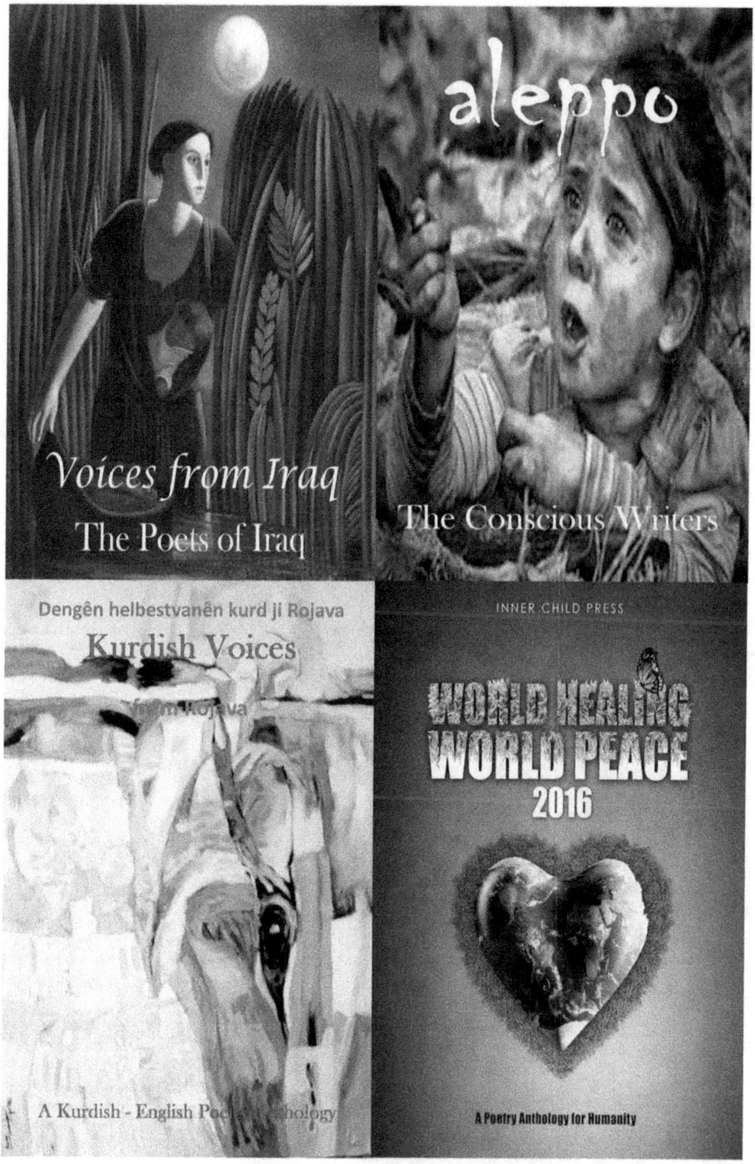

Now Available

www.innerchildpress.com/anthologies

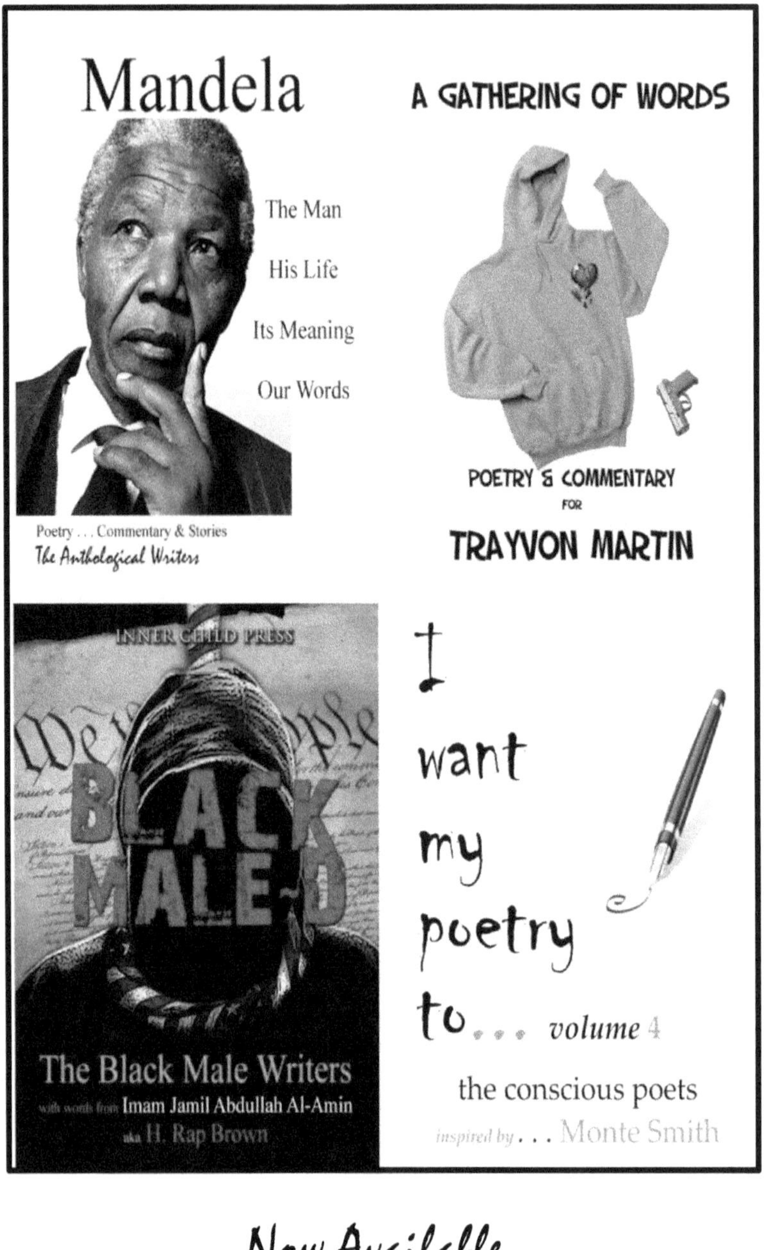

Now Available

www.innerchildpress.com/anthologies

Now Available

www.innerchildpress.com/anthologies

Now Available

www.innerchildpress.com/anthologies

Now Available

www.innerchildpress.com/anthologies

Now Available

www.innerchildpress.com/the-year-of-the-poet

Now Available

www.innerchildpress.com/the-year-of-the-poet

Now Available

www.innerchildpress.com/the-year-of-the-poet

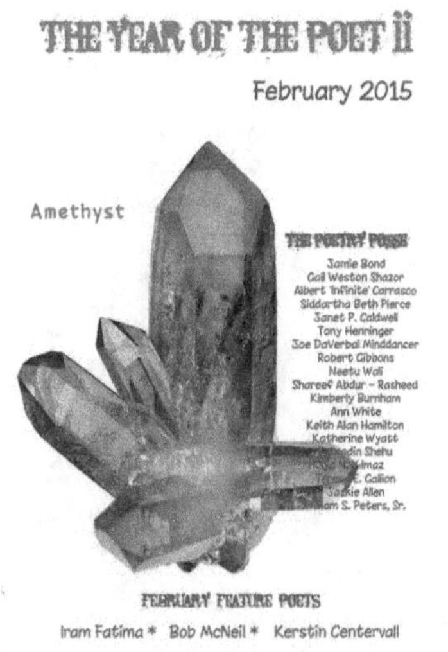

Now Available

www.innerchildpress.com/the-year-of-the-poet

The Year of the Poet II
May 2015
May's Featured Poets
Emeralds
The Poetry Posse 2015
Siddartha Beth Pierce * Janet P. Caldwell * Tony Henninger
Joe DaVerbal Minddancer * Neetu Wali * Shareef Abdur – Rasheed
Kimberly Burnham * Ann White * Keith Alan Hamilton
Katherine Wyatt * Fahredin Shehu * Hülya N. Yılmaz
Teresa E. Gallion * Jackie Allen * William S. Peters, Sr.

The Year of the Poet II
June 2015
June's Featured Poets
Pearl
The Poetry Posse 2015
Jamie Bond * Gail Weston Shazor * Albert 'Infinite' Carrasco
Siddartha Beth Pierce * Janet P. Caldwell * Tony Henninger
Joe DaVerbal Minddancer * Neetu Wali * Shareef Abdur – Rasheed
Kimberly Burnham * Ann White * Keith Alan Hamilton
Katherine Wyatt * Fahredin Shehu * Hülya N. Yılmaz
Teresa E. Gallion * Jackie Allen * William S. Peters, Sr

The Year of the Poet II
July 2015
The Featured Poets for July 2015
Abhik Shome * Christina Neal * Robert Neal
Rubies
The Poetry Posse 2015
Jamie Bond * Gail Weston Shazor * Albert 'Infinite' Carrasco
Siddartha Beth Pierce * Janet P. Caldwell * Tony Henninger
Joe DaVerbal Minddancer * Neetu Wali * Shareef Abdur – Rasheed
Kimberly Burnham * Ann White * Keith Alan Hamilton
Katherine Wyatt * Fahredin Shehu * Hülya N. Yılmaz
Teresa E. Gallion * Jackie Allen * William S. Peters, Sr

The Year of the Poet II
August 2015
Peridot
Featured Poets
Gayle Howell
Ann Chalasz
Christopher Schultz
The Poetry Posse 2015
Jamie Bond * Gail Weston Shazor * Albert 'Infinite' Carrasco
Siddartha Beth Pierce * Janet P. Caldwell * Tony Henninger
Joe DaVerbal Minddancer * Neetu Wali * Shareef Abdur – Rasheed
Kimberly Burnham * Ann White * Keith Alan Hamilton
Katherine Wyatt * Fahredin Shehu * Hülya N. Yılmaz
Teresa E. Gallion * Jackie Allen * William S. Peters, Sr

Now Available

www.innerchildpress.com/the-year-of-the-poet

Now Available

www.innerchildpress.com/the-year-of-the-poet

Now Available

www.innerchildpress.com/the-year-of-the-poet

Now Available

www.innerchildpress.com/the-year-of-the-poet

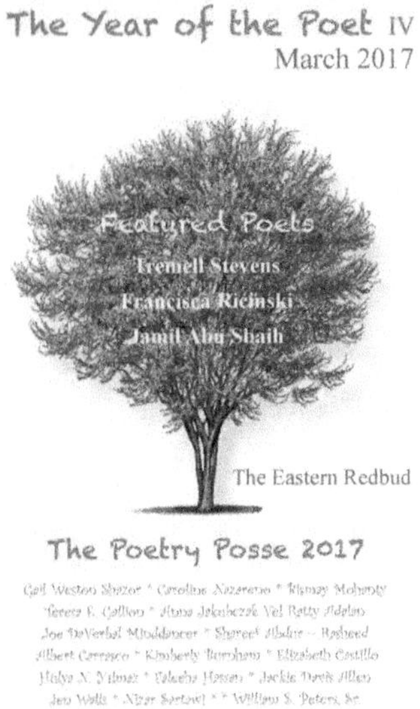

Now Available

www.innerchildpress.com/the-year-of-the-poet

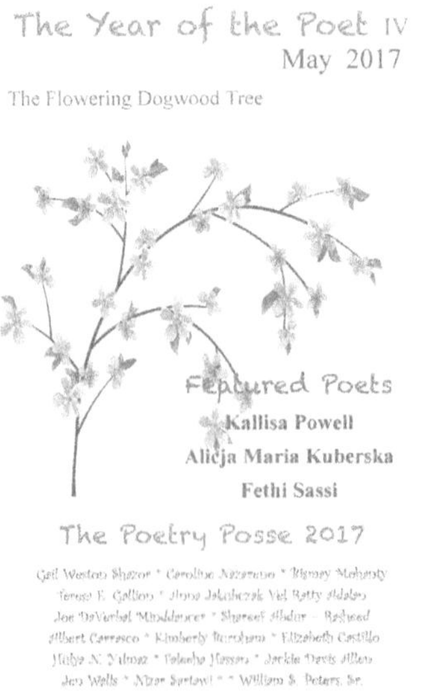

Now Available

www.innerchildpress.com/the-year-of-the-poet

The Year of the Poet IV
September 2017

Featured Poets

Martina Reisz Newberry

Ameer Nassir

Christine Fulco Neal

Robert Neal

The Elm Tree

The Poetry Posse 2017

Gail Weston Shazor * Caroline Nazareno * Bismay Mohanty
Teresa E. Gallion * Anna Jakubczak Vel Ratty Adalan
Joe DaVerbal Minddancer * Shareef Abdur – Rasheed
Albert Carrasco * Kimberly Burnham * Elizabeth Castillo
Hülya N. Yılmaz * Faleeha Hassan * Jackie Davis Allen
Jen Walls * Nizar Sartawi * * William S. Peters, Sr.

The Year of the Poet IV
October 2017

Featured Poets

Ahmed Abu Saleem

Nedal Al-Qaeim

Sadeddin Shahin

The Black Walnut Tree

The Poetry Posse 2017

Gail Weston Shazor * Caroline Nazareno * Bismay Mohanty
Teresa E. Gallion * Anna Jakubczak Vel Ratty Adalan
Joe DaVerbal Minddancer * Shareef Abdur – Rasheed
Albert Carrasco * Kimberly Burnham * Elizabeth Castillo
Hülya N. Yılmaz * Faleeha Hassan * Jackie Davis Allen
Jen Walls * Nizar Sartawi * * William S. Peters, Sr.

The Year of the Poet IV
November 2017

Featured Poets

Kay Peters

Alfreda D. Ghee

Gabriella Garofalo

Rosemary Cappello

The Tree of Life

The Poetry Posse 2017

Gail Weston Shazor * Caroline Nazareno * Bismay Mohanty
Teresa E. Gallion * Anna Jakubczak Vel Ratty Adalan
Joe DaVerbal Minddancer * Shareef Abdur – Rasheed
Albert Carrasco * Kimberly Burnham * Elizabeth Castillo
Hülya N. Yılmaz * Faleeha Hassan * Jackie Davis Allen
Jen Walls * Nizar Sartawi * William S. Peters, Sr.

The Year of the Poet IV
December 2017

Featured Poets

Justice Clarke

Mariel M. Pabroa

Kiley Brown

The Fig Tree

The Poetry Posse 2017

Gail Weston Shazor * Caroline Nazareno * Bismay Mohanty
Teresa E. Gallion * Anna Jakubczak Vel Ratty Adalan
Joe DaVerbal Minddancer * Shareef Abdur – Rasheed
Albert Carrasco * Kimberly Burnham * Elizabeth Castillo
Hülya N. Yılmaz * Faleeha Hassan * Jackie Davis Allen
Jen Walls * Nizar Sartawi * William S. Peters, Sr.

Now Available

www.innerchildpress.com/the-year-of-the-poet

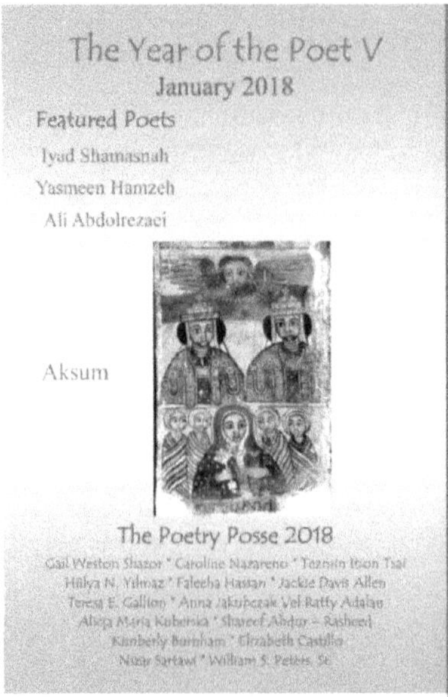

Now Available

www.innerchildpress.com/the-year-of-the-poet

The Year of the Poet V
May 2018
Featured Poets
The Sumerians
The Poetry Posse 2018
Gail Weston Shazor * Nizar Sartawi * Hülya N. Yılmaz
Jackie Davis Allen * Caroline 'Ceri' Nazareno
Alicja Maria Kuberska * Teresa E. Gallion
Kimberly Burnham * Shareef Abdur – Rasheed
Faleeha Hassan * Elizabeth Castillo * Swapna Behera
Tezmin Ition Tsai * William S. Peters, Sr.

The Year of the Poet V
June 2018
Featured Poets
Briell Maliqi * Daim Miftari * Gojko Božović * Sofija Živković
The Paleo Indians
The Poetry Posse 2018

The Year of the Poet V
July 2018
Featured Poets
Padmaja Iyengar-Paddy
Mohammad Ikbal Harb
Eliza Segiet
Tom Higgins
Oceania
The Poetry Posse 2018
Gail Weston Shazor * Nizar Sartawi * Hülya N. Yılmaz
Jackie Davis Allen * Caroline 'Ceri' Nazareno
Alicja Maria Kuberska * Teresa E. Gallion
Kimberly Burnham * Shareef Abdur – Rasheed
Faleeha Hassan * Elizabeth Castillo * Swapna Behera
Tezmin Ition Tsai * William S. Peters, Sr.

The Year of the Poet V
August 2018
Featured Poets
Hussein Habasch * Mircea Dan Duta * Naida Mujkić * Swagat Das
The Lapita
The Poetry Posse 2018
Gail Weston Shazor * Nizar Sartawi * Hülya N. Yılmaz
Jackie Davis Allen * Caroline 'Ceri' Nazareno
Alicja Maria Kuberska * Teresa E. Gallion
Kimberly Burnham * Shareef Abdur – Rasheed
Ashok K. Bhargava* Elizabeth Castillo * Swapna Behaera
Tezmin Ition Tsai * William S. Peters, Sr.

Now Available

www.innerchildpress.com/the-year-of-the-poet

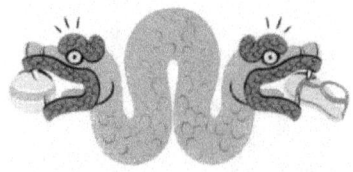

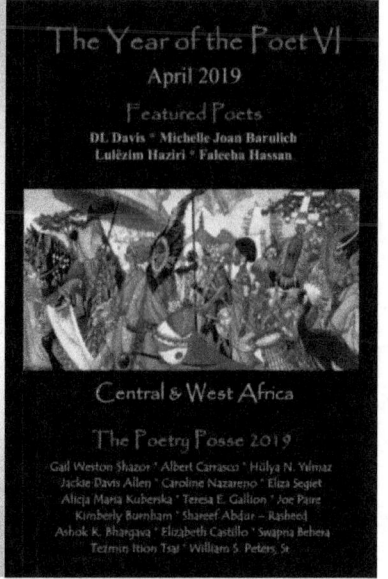

Now Available

www.innerchildpress.com/the-year-of-the-poet

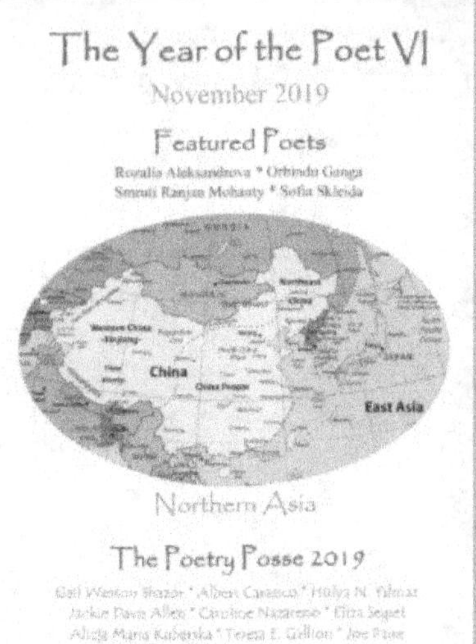

Now Available

www.innerchildpress.com/the-year-of-the-poet

Now Available

www.innerchildpress.com/the-year-of-the-poet

The Year of the Poet VII
May 2020
Featured Poets
Alok Kumar Ray * Eden S. Trinidad
Franco Barbato * Izabela Zubko
Ralph Bunche ~ 1950
The Year of Peace
Celebrating past Nobel Peace Prize Recipients
The Poetry Posse 2020
Gail Weston Shazor * Albert Carasco * Hülya N. Yilmaz
Jackie Davis Allen * Caroline Nazareno * Eliza Segiet
Alicja Maria Kuberska * Teresa E. Gallion * Joe Paire
Kimberly Burnham * Shareef Abdur – Rasheed
Ashok K. Bhargava * Elizabeth Castillo * Swapna Behera
Tezmin Ition Tsai * William S. Peters, Sr.
The Year of the Poet VII
June 2020
Featured Poets
Eftichia Kapardeli * Metin Cengiz
Hussein Habasch * Kosh K Mathew
Albert John Lutuli ~ 1960
The Year of Peace
Celebrating past Nobel Peace Prize Recipients
The Poetry Posse 2020
Gail Weston Shazor * Albert Carasco * Hülya N. Yilmaz
Jackie Davis Allen * Caroline Nazareno * Eliza Segiet
Alicja Maria Kuberska * Teresa E. Gallion * Joe Paire
Kimberly Burnham * Shareef Abdur – Rasheed
Ashok K. Bhargava * Elizabeth Castillo * Swapna Behera
Tezmin Ition Tsai * William S. Peters, Sr.
The Year of the Poet VII
July 2020
Featured Poets
Mykola Martyniuk * Orbindu Ganga
Roula Pollard * Kam Praktisha
Norman Ernest Borlaug ~ 1970
The Year of Peace
Celebrating past Nobel Peace Prize Recipients
The Poetry Posse 2020
Gail Weston Shazor * Albert Carasco * Hülya N. Yilmaz
Jackie Davis Allen * Caroline Nazareno * Eliza Segiet
Alicja Maria Kuberska * Teresa E. Gallion * Joe Paire
Kimberly Burnham * Shareef Abdur – Rasheed
Ashok K. Bhargava * Elizabeth Castillo * Swapna Behera
Tezmin Ition Tsai * William S. Peters, Sr.
The Year of the Poet VII
August 2020
Featured Poets
Dr Pragya Suman * Chinh Nguyen
Srinivas Vasudev * Ugwu Leonard Ifeanyi, Jr.
Adolfo Pérez Esquivel ~ 1980
The Year of Peace
Celebrating past Nobel Peace Prize Recipients
The Poetry Posse 2020
Gail Weston Shazor * Albert Carasco * Hülya N. Yilmaz
Jackie Davis Allen * Caroline Nazareno * Eliza Segiet
Alicja Maria Kuberska * Teresa E. Gallion * Joe Paire
Kimberly Burnham * Shareef Abdur – Rasheed
Ashok K. Bhargava * Elizabeth Castillo * Swapna Behera
Tezmin Ition Tsai * William S. Peters, Sr.

Now Available

www.innerchildpress.com/the-year-of-the-poet

The Year of the Poet VIII
January 2021
Featured Global Poets
Andrew Scott * Debaprasanna Biswas
Shakil Kalam * Changming Yuan
Banksy's The Girl with the Pierced Eardrum
Poetry . . . Ekphrasticly Speaking
The Poetry Posse 2020
Gail Weston Shazor * Albert Carassco * Hülya N. Yılmaz
Jackie Davis Allen * Caroline Nazareno * Eliza Segiet
Alicja Maria Kuberska * Teresa E. Gallion * Joe Paire
Kimberly Burnham * Shareef Abdur – Rasheed
Ashok K. Bhargava * Elizabeth Castillo * Swapna Behera
Tezmin Ition Tsai * William S. Peters, Sr.

The Year of the Poet VIII
February 2021
Featured Global Poets
T. Ramesh Babu * Ruchida Barman
Neptune Barman * Faleeha Hassan
Emory Douglas : 1968 Olympics mural
Poetry . . . Ekphrasticly Speaking
The Poetry Posse 2021
Gail Weston Shazor * Albert Carassco * Hülya N. Yılmaz
Jackie Davis Allen * Caroline Nazareno * Eliza Segiet
Alicja Maria Kuberska * Teresa E. Gallion * Joe Paire
Kimberly Burnham * Shareef Abdur – Rasheed
Ashok K. Bhargava * Elizabeth Castillo * Swapna Behera
Tezmin Ition Tsai * William S. Peters, Sr.

The Year of the Poet VIII
March 2021
Featured Global Poets
Claudia Piccinno * Mohammed Jabr
Luzviminda Rivera *Nigar Arif
Tatyana Fazlalizadeh
Poetry . . . Ekphrasticly Speaking
The Poetry Posse 2021

The Year of the Poet VIII
April 2021
Featured Global Poets
Katarzyna Brus- Sawczuk * Anwesha Paul
Rozalia Aleksandrova * Shahid Abbas
Pablo O'Higgins
Poetry . . . Ekphrasticly Speaking
The Poetry Posse 2021
Gail Weston Shazor * Albert Carassco * Hülya N. Yılmaz
Jackie Davis Allen * Caroline Nazareno * Eliza Segiet
Alicja Maria Kuberska * Teresa E. Gallion * Joe Paire
Kimberly Burnham * Shareef Abdur – Rasheed
Ashok K. Bhargava * Elizabeth Castillo * Swapna Behera
Tezmin Ition Tsai * William S. Peters, Sr.

Now Available

www.innerchildpress.com/the-year-of-the-poet

Now Available

www.innerchildpress.com/the-year-of-the-poet

The Year of the Poet IX
January 2022
Featured Global Poets
Ratan Ghosh * Christine Neil-Wright
Andrew Scott * Ashok Kumar
Climate Change : The Ice Cap
Poetry . . . Ekphrasticly Speaking
The Poetry Posse 2021
Gail Weston Shazor * Albert Carassco * Hülya N. Yılmaz
Jackie Davis Allen * Caroline Nazareno * Eliza Segiet
Alicja Maria Kuberska * Teresa E. Gallion * Joe Paire
Kimberly Burnham * Shareef Abdur – Rasheed
Ashok K. Bhargava * Elizabeth Castillo * Swapna Behera
Tezmin Ition Tsai * William S. Peters, Sr.

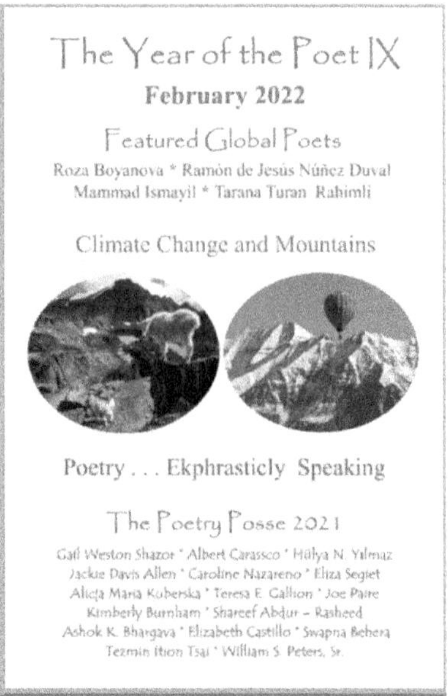
The Year of the Poet IX
February 2022
Featured Global Poets
Roza Boyanova * Ramòn de Jesùs Núñez Duval
Mammad Ismayil * Tarana Turan Rahimli
Climate Change and Mountains
Poetry . . . Ekphrasticly Speaking
The Poetry Posse 2021
Gail Weston Shazor * Albert Carassco * Hülya N. Yılmaz
Jackie Davis Allen * Caroline Nazareno * Eliza Segiet
Alicja Maria Kuberska * Teresa E. Gallion * Joe Paire
Kimberly Burnham * Shareef Abdur – Rasheed
Ashok K. Bhargava * Elizabeth Castillo * Swapna Behera
Tezmin Ition Tsai * William S. Peters, Sr.

The Year of the Poet IX
March 2022
Featured Global Poets
Dimitris P. Kraniotis * Marlene Pasini
Kennedy Ochieng * Swayam Prashant
Climate Change and Space Debris
Poetry . . . Ekphrasticly Speaking
The Poetry Posse 2021

The Year of the Poet IX
April 2022
Featured Global Poets
Alonzo Gross * Dr. Debaprasanna Biswas
Monsif Beroual * Carol Aronoff
Climate Change and Oceans
*Celebrating our 100th Edition *
Poetry . . . Ekphrasticly Speaking
The Poetry Posse 2021
Gail Weston Shazor * Albert Carassco * Hülya N. Yılmaz
Jackie Davis Allen * Caroline Nazareno * Eliza Segiet
Alicja Maria Kuberska * Teresa E. Gallion * Joe Paire
Kimberly Burnham * Shareef Abdur – Rasheed
Ashok K. Bhargava * Elizabeth Castillo * Swapna Behera
Tezmin Ition Tsai * William S. Peters, Sr.

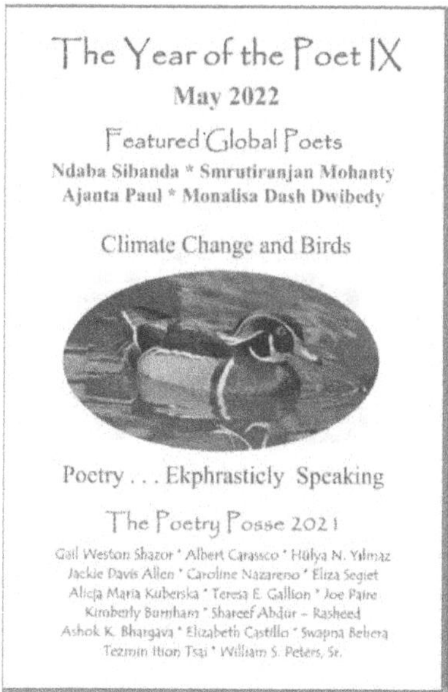

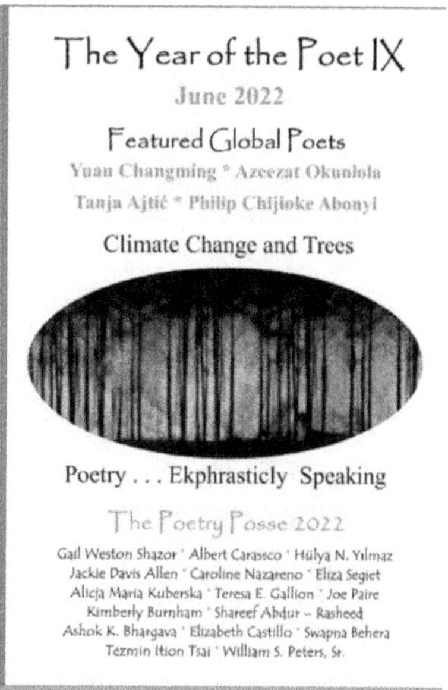

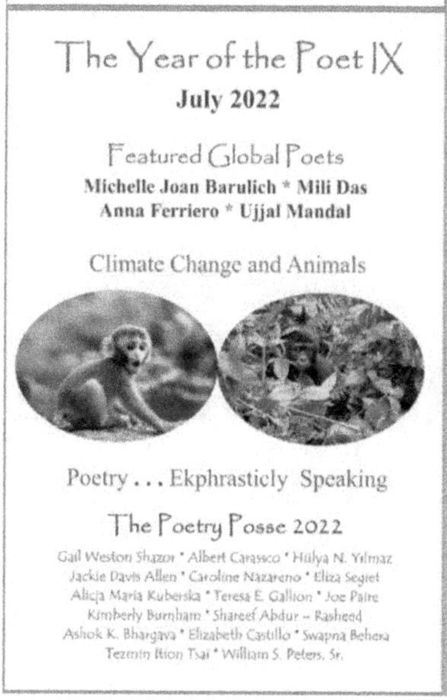

Now Available

www.innerchildpress.com/the-year-of-the-poet

Now Available

www.innerchildpress.com/the-year-of-the-poet

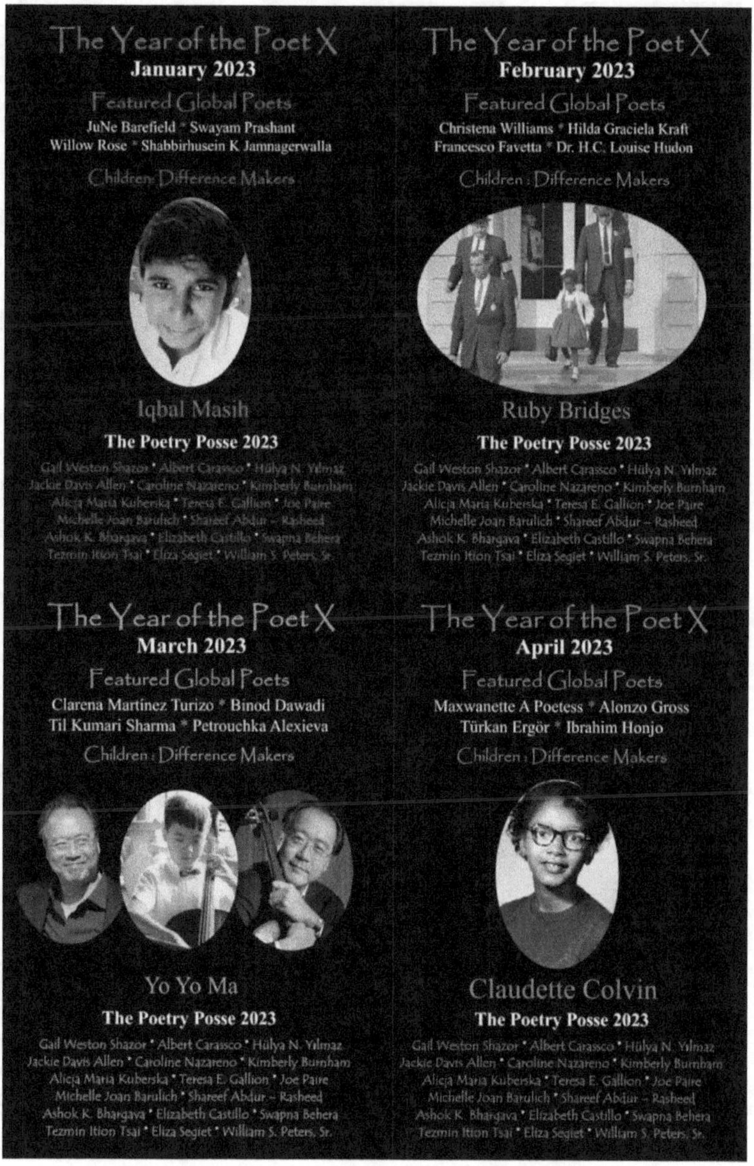

Now Available

www.innerchildpress.com/the-year-of-the-poet

Now Available

www.innerchildpress.com/the-year-of-the-poet

Now Available

www.innerchildpress.com/the-year-of-the-poet

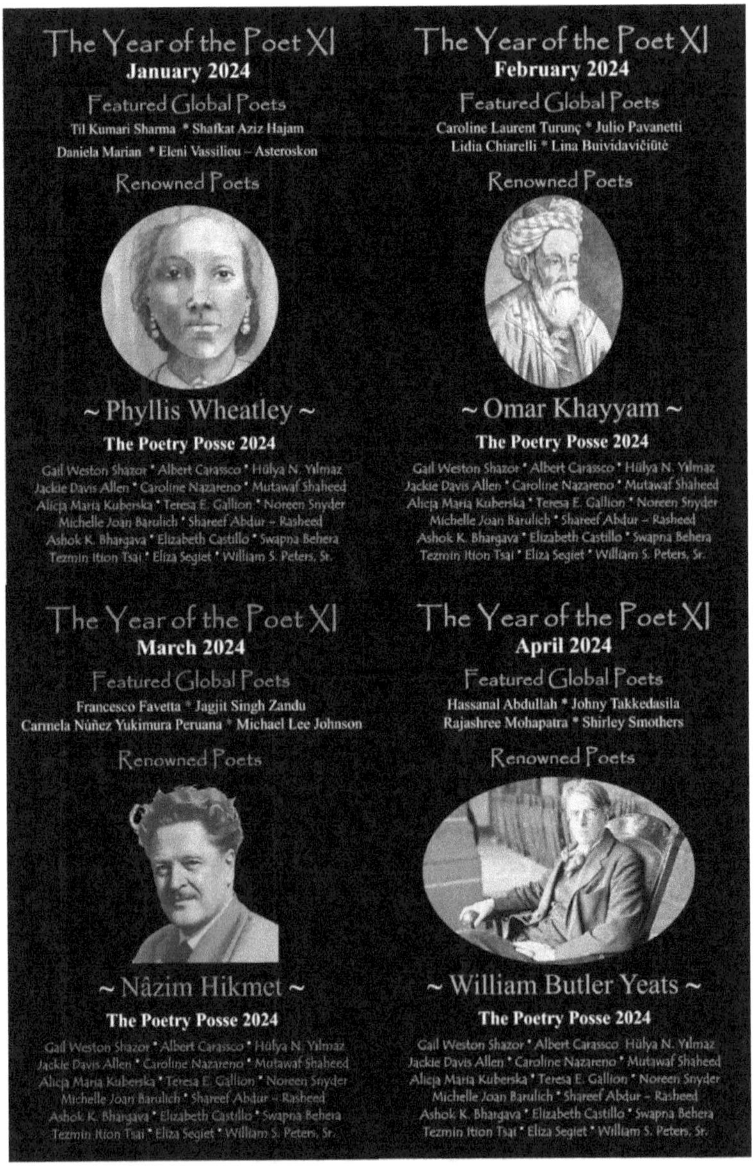

Now Available

www.innerchildpress.com/the-year-of-the-poet

Inner Child Press Anthologies

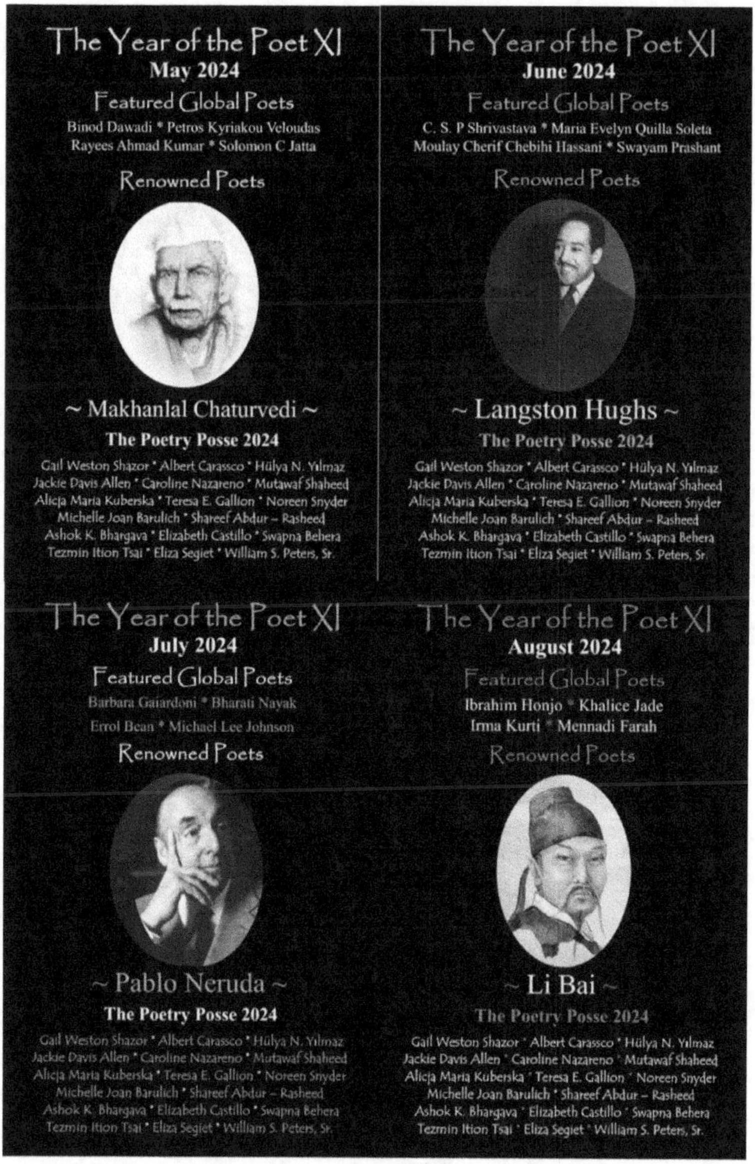

Now Available

www.innerchildpress.com/the-year-of-the-poet

and there is much, much more !

visit . . .

www.innerchildpress.com/anthologies-sales-special.php

Also check out our Authors and all the wonderful Books Available at :

www.innerchildpress.com/authors-pages

Now Available

www.worldhealingworldpeacepoetry.com

Now Available

www.worldhealingworldpeacepoetry.com

www.worldhealingworldpeacepoetry.com

World Healing World Peace

Poetry

i am a believer!

World Healing
World Peace

2012, 2014, 2016, 2018, 2020, 2022

Now Available

www.worldhealingworldpeacepoetry.com

Inner Child Press International

'building bridges of cultural understanding'

Meet the Board of Directors

William S. Peters, Sr.
Chair Person
Founder
Inner Child Enterprises
Inner Child Press

Hülya N Yılmaz
Director
Editing Services
Co-Chair Person

Fahredin B. Shehu
Director
Cultural Affairs

Elizabeth E. Castillo
Director
Recording Secretary

De'Andre Hawthorne
Director
Performance Poetry

Gail Weston Shazor
Director
Anthologies

Kimberly Burnham
Director
Cultural Ambassador
Pacific Northwest
USA

Ashok K. Bhargava
Director
WINAwards

Deborah Smart
Director
Publicity
Marketing

www.innerchildpress.com

This Anthological Publication
is underwritten solely by

Inner Child Press International

Inner Child Press is a Publishing Company Founded and Operated by Writers. Our personal publishing experiences provides us an intimate understanding of the sometimes daunting challenges Writers, New and Seasoned may face in the Business of Publishing and Marketing their Creative "Written Work".

For more Information

Inner Child Press International

www.innerchildpress.com

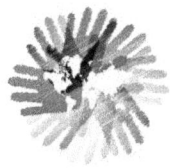

~ *fini* ~

www.ingramcontent.com/pod-product-compliance
Lightning Source LLC
LaVergne TN
LVHW051041080426
835508LV00019B/1637
* 9 7 8 1 9 6 1 4 9 8 4 3 3 *